# READING THE TEN COMMANDMENTS ANEW

# BY THE SAME AUTHOR:

*The Pilgrim God: A Biblical Journey*
(Washington: The Pastoral Press, 1985 / Dublin: Veritas, 1990)

*The Way of the Lord: A New Testament Pilgrimage*
(The Pastoral Press / Veritas, 1990)

*Praying the Our Father Today*
(The Pastoral Press, 1992)

*God of the Unexpected*
(London: Geoffrey Chapman / Mowbray, 1995)

*The Adventure of Holiness:*
*Biblical Foundations and Present-Day Perspectives*
(New York: ST PAULS / Alba House, 1999)

*At the Wellspring: Jesus and the Samaritan Woman*
(New York: ST PAULS / Alba House, 2001)

Visit our website at
WWW.ALBAHOUSE.ORG

or call 1-800-343-2522 (ALBA)
and request current catalog

# Reading the Ten Commandments Anew

## Towards a Land of Freedom

BROTHER JOHN OF TAIZÉ

ST PAULS

# Alba House

Originally published in French by Ateliers et Presses de Taizé, Taizé-Communauté, France, 2002, under the title
*Vers une terre de liberté: Une relecture des dix commandments.*


Library of Congress Cataloging-in-Publication Data

John de Taizé, frère.
  [Vers une terre de liberté. English]
    Reading the Ten commandments anew: towards a land of freedom /
Brother John of Taizé.
      p. cm.
    ISBN 0-8189-0955-2
1. Ten commandments. 2. Youth—Religious life.  I. Title

  BV4655.J6213 2003
  241.5'2—dc21                               2003008189


Produced and designed in the United States of America by the
Fathers and Brothers of the Society of St. Paul,
2187 Victory Boulevard, Staten Island, New York 10314-6603,
as part of their communications apostolate.


ISBN: 0-8189-0955-2

**Printing Information:**

Current Printing - first digit   1    2    3    4    5    6    7    8    9    10

Year of Current Printing - first year shown

2004    2005    2006    2007    2008    2009    2010    2011    2012    2013

# Contents

I run along the way of your commandments,
for you have set my heart free.

(Psalm 119:32)

# Introduction

Why write a book on the Ten Commandments?

Every year, in preparing the Bible introductions I will give to the young adults who participate in the international meetings on the hill of Taizé, I look for a topic that can structure the week and help participants to see connections between the different parts of Scripture. Sometimes this topic is a particular notion such as "holiness" or "newness"; at other times we read together a biblical text and attempt to understand it in greater depth. More than once I have found that reflecting on a well-known passage, such as the Our Father or the Beatitudes, is a particularly fruitful endeavor. These are key passages for the understanding of the Christian message, and therefore the very act of rereading them, of coming to grips with them as if they had something new to tell us, involves a growth in faith. When we think that we already "know" something, that we have understood it adequately and have essentially nothing more to learn from it, in a sense that reality has ceased to exist for us and has simply taken its place as part of the furniture of our inner world. While the impression to have already understood may not always be of such great import when we are dealing with ordinary human notions, it leads to a serious misunderstanding when applied to the truths of biblical faith. For believers, the Bible is not just a collection of human words, stories and attitudes; through these human realities, in inexplicable fashion, we come into contact with the living God, who is by definition beyond all we can grasp with our human powers. This is in fact the most profound dynamic of the Bible: God uses what is already at our disposition to lead us to where we have never yet been, to a life beyond all our dreams. As an age-old Christian text expresses it in a slightly different context, through what is visible to our eyes we are taken hold of and led to love the invisible God (*ut per [visibilia] in invisibilium amorem rapiamur*, Preface for the Nativity of Christ).

This book, then, proposes to undertake a rereading of another of those well-known biblical texts, indeed for some people the best known of all: the Ten Commandments. This proposition may well awaken a resistance in even the most well disposed reader. The Ten Commandments transport most of us back to the religion of our childhood, to catechism class or Sunday school. They easily evoke blind obedience, sin and guilt, a moralistic or legalistic mindset; their negative approach seems to be at the opposite extreme from the positive religion of love and responsibility which we identify with Jesus Christ. Unless, of course, we take the opposite tack, and welcome a return to "that old-time religion" as a bulwark against the tidal wave of relativism and cultural anarchy that seems about to engulf us. If we are guided by our spontaneous reactions, in short, we risk rejecting or accepting this passage for reasons that have more to do with our own preconceptions than with its meaning in the context of the biblical message as a whole.

A first step beyond this dilemma might be to realize that the Ten Commandments are not as familiar to us as we imagine. First of all, when we open the Bible, we quickly notice that the version we learned as children does not correspond exactly to the words we find there. Our first surprise may be to discover that there are not one but two versions of the Ten Commandments, given in two separate books of the Bible: chapter 20 of the Book of Exodus and chapter 5 of the Book of Deuteronomy. While these two versions agree in most respects, there are some small and not-so-small differences between them. The same thing is true, incidentally, for those other two key Bible passages mentioned above — in the Gospels according to Matthew and Luke, we find two independent versions of both the Lord's Prayer and the Beatitudes. Although at first we may view this fact as unfortunate, upon deeper reflection we can see that it opens up vistas that are truly liberating. By witnessing to the impossibility of a literal, word-by-word interpretation of biblical truth — we simply do not know the exact words of Jesus or of God's revelation on Sinai, and never shall — it frees us to go towards the truth which the words point to without being able to capture perfectly. To use the language of Saint Paul, we are thus led to follow not the letter but the spirit, *for the letter kills, but the Spirit gives life* (2 Corinthians 3:6). This "spirit," of course, is not mere human fantasizing but rather the Holy Spirit of God, shining through the inspired writings and present in the community of believers as they attempt to understand the faith they have received and see its relevance for their day.

In the second place, the expression "the ten commandments" is found nowhere in Scripture itself. What we have are a few texts that speak in the following way:

The Lord said to Moses, "Write down these words, because in accordance with these words I have made a covenant with you and with Israel." And he was there with the Lord forty days and forty nights. He ate no bread and drank no water. And he wrote on the tablets the words of the covenant, the ten words.

(Exodus 34:27-28; see also Deuteronomy 4:13; 10:4)

Although some of the English translations render the final expression as "the ten commandments," which seems to be less a translation than an interpretation based on a preconceived notion, the Hebrew has *'asheret ha-debarim*, "the ten words." In fact, a more accurate rendering in English would be "the ten sayings" or "the ten statements," since it is clear from the context that we are dealing not with single words but with complete utterances. The Greek version of the Bible translated this as τα δεκα ρηματα (*ta deka rhêmata*) or οι δεκα λογοι (*hoi deka logoi*), from which we get the expression "the Decalogue," which is often used as a more technical synonym for the Ten Commandments. Henceforth, then, we shall use the expression the TEN WORDS in this book, placing it in capitals to avoid any confusion with the normal meaning of "word." This nuance is not without its importance: although God's Word has performative power, in that it tends towards the realization of what it enunciates, an utterance is clearly not the same thing as a commandment, and a too-facile identification of faith with morality does not help people today to grasp the true identity of the biblical God and God's relationship to the created universe.

The texts mentioned above seem to bear witness to an ancient tradition, preserved in the foundational writings of the people of Israel, that their relationship with God involved the communication of ten sayings inscribed on stone tablets. Why ten, we might ask, and not seven, say, or twelve, both biblical numbers with a strong claim to significance? The answer remains shrouded in the mists of time. Perhaps it was a simple mnemonic device based on the fingers of both hands. The real problem posed by this tradition is in fact not the absolute number of the sayings, but how the number ten fits with the text handed down to us. It is admittedly not easy to extract precisely ten sayings from Exodus 20 or Deuteronomy 5. This is shown by the fact that historically there are at least three different ways of dividing the text: one goes back to Saint Augustine and has been accepted by the Catholic and Lutheran churches; a second, older system is used by Reformed and Orthodox Christians; a third, finally, is found in the Jewish tradition. One group's "fifth commandment" is another group's "fourth," and so on. In short, although for everyone the TEN WORDS is equivalent to the text received on Mount Sinai as the prologue to the Law of Moses, this identification is problematic, at any rate if we take the number ten literally. This leads us by another route to suppose that the received text has been reworked and expanded in the course of its history. Things are not quite as clear as a naïve reading would have it; there is significant room for interpretation.

We should mention a final preconception that makes our access to the text still more complicated. One often encounters the assertion, sometimes in authoritative writings, that the Ten Commandments are a kind of "natural law" valid for human beings in all times and places, a universal foundation for ethics obvious to all people of good will and independent of belief in a particular god or in a specific revelation. It is certainly true that part of the text seems to fit such a description. The command not to kill one's fellow human beings or steal from them, for example, lies at the root of life in any society. If we examine the structure of the passage as a whole, however, we notice that the heart of the TEN WORDS is the injunction regarding the Sabbath. This is both the central section and the longest of all. Now it should be clear that this particular WORD is a pure act of revelation: not only is it incomprehensible outside of Israel, but even for God's people it could never have been rationally deduced from a more general truth about the deity, although attempts in this direction have not been lacking. The saying concerning the Sabbath points rather in the opposite direction: through it we encounter a "particular" God who is the Source of Israel's life and who cannot be subsumed under more comprehensive religious or ethical categories. The TEN WORDS are thus ultimately comprehensible only in the context of a revelation inseparable from a particular history, the one recounted in the Bible. What is universal in them finds its meaning by being a part of this history. Their most authentic significance is not atemporal or ahistorical; unlike a philosophical teaching, the universality of the TEN WORDS cannot be grasped by abstracting from the historical context that brought them into being. It is to that context that we now turn, as the first step in elucidating their meaning.

READING THE TEN COMMANDMENTS ANEW

I am the Lord* your God, who brought
you out from the land of Egypt,
from the house of servitude.

(Exodus 20:2 / Deuteronomy 5:6)

---

\* Following the Jewish practice, the expression "the Lord" is used to replace
YHWH, the unspoken Name of God.

In the Jewish tradition, this is the first of the TEN WORDS. And perhaps to our great surprise, it is not a commandment. So much for the notion, unfortunately still common among Christians, that the Jewish religion is a legalistic religion of blind obedience, while for their part they enjoy the untrammeled freedom of the Spirit. In reality, far from telling us what we need to do to earn God's good graces, the first WORD tells us simply who God is and what God has done for us. To use a later Christian distinction, it is not "law" but "gospel."

The entire Bible, in fact, begins with that mystery at the heart of existence that we call God. It is not first of all an instruction book as to how humans should act. God's identity and activity always come first, and human beings can do absolutely nothing to merit the attention and compassionate care God bestows on them. Many people are familiar with this truth as it is formulated in the pages of the New Testament. Saint John states it most succinctly:

> This is love: not that we loved God, but that God loved
> us and sent his Son as a source of forgiveness for our
> sins.... We should love, because God loved us first.
> (1 John 4:10, 19)

Saint Paul, in his turn, says the same thing in a different language:

> When we were incapable of doing good, Christ died
> at the appropriate time for those without God. Some-
> one might with difficulty die for a person of integrity.

Yes, for a good person someone might just dare to give their life. But God showed the quality of his love for us in that Christ died for us while we were still sinners.

(Romans 5:6-8)

God loved us first, before we were able or willing to do anything to deserve or earn that love. All that we do can only be a consequence of, or even better a response to, the utterly free gift of God. If this is the heart of the Christian Gospel, it is important to realize that the very same logic presides at the founding event of the people of Israel, the exodus from Egypt. At the beginning of the TEN WORDS, God defines himself as the One who comes to liberate suffering humanity from the bonds that keep them captive.

The Lord said, "I have seen clearly the misery of my people in Egypt and heard their cry of distress in the presence of their slave-drivers. Yes, I have become acquainted with their suffering. I have come down to save them from the power of the Egyptians and to bring them up from this land to a good and spacious land, a land flowing with milk and honey...."

(Exodus 3:7-8a)

And to avoid any ambiguity, a passage from the Book of Deuteronomy states clearly that nothing Israel had done determined the divine activity in advance. It was pure gratuitousness, an unconditional expression of God's generosity and faithfulness.

For you are a people holy to the Lord your God. The Lord your God chose you to become his people, his

4

personal property out of all the peoples on the face of the earth. The Lord did not show his love for you and choose you because you were the most numerous of all peoples, for you were the smallest of all peoples. But it was because of the Lord's love for you, and because he kept the oath he swore to your ancestors, that the Lord brought you out with deeds of power and redeemed you from the house of servitude, from the power of Pharaoh, king of Egypt.

(Deuteronomy 7:6-8)

Any talk of divine commands and human obligations can therefore only come in the second place, as a human response to God's utterly free choice. Another key text from the Book of Deuteronomy expresses this logic while explaining how the nation's creed is transmitted from one generation to the next:

In the future, when your son asks you, "What is the meaning of the instructions, decrees and judgments which the Lord your God has prescribed for you?" you will say to your son, "Once we were slaves of Pharaoh in Egypt, and the Lord brought us out of Egypt with deeds of power. The Lord worked great and terrible signs and wonders in our sight against Egypt, against Pharaoh and his entire household. And he brought us out from there in order to lead us to the land he had promised on oath to give to our ancestors. And the Lord has commanded us to observe all these decrees and to respect the Lord our God, to be happy in all our days and to have life, as we have today. For us, right living will be to observe and to keep all these commands before the Lord our God as he has commanded us." (Deuteronomy 6:20-25)

As in the TEN WORDS, the father's reply to his child's question begins by recalling God's act of liberation and the gift of a homeland; human activity is clearly situated in the wake of the divine initiative. But the text adds a further important precision: the commandments must be followed in order to have life and happiness in the land given by God. Human beings are not robots, and so it cannot be enough for God to give life and freedom by a unilateral act or decree. For that gift to become operative, the beneficiaries must translate it into the concrete circumstances of their existence. The gift must become a way of life.

In Exodus 34:28, the TEN WORDS are also called *the words of the covenant,* and in fact the biblical notion of covenant offers the clearest context for understanding God's law in general and the TEN WORDS in particular. In the Hebrew Scriptures, this text is attached to an event which took place on a holy mountain (Sinai in Exodus, Horeb in Deuteronomy) shortly after the Israelites left Egypt. On that mountain, the Lord revealed his identity as the God who liberated a band of former slaves and then offered them a covenant in order to make of them a people. In the world of the ancient Middle East, the word *berith,* often translated as "covenant" but which has in fact several different meanings, can refer to an agreement or pact between two parties. There were different kinds of covenants, but the one used as an analogy for the relationship between the Lord and Israel seems to be a type of agreement that was made between a powerful king or nation and a weaker vassal. In exchange for guaranteeing the identity and security of the client state, the king asked the vassal to behave in a way consonant with his protection. The pact was reciprocal, but the partners were not equal. This model had the advantage of giving form to the relationship between Israel and its God, although at the same time it is important to recognize that there are unique aspects of that ongoing relationship which cannot be subsumed under the logic of any human agreement.

When those who have escaped from Egypt reach Sinai, they receive through Moses the following communication from God:

> Moses went up to God, and the Lord called to him from the mountain, saying, "Say this to the House of Jacob and tell the children of Israel: 'You have seen what I did to the Egyptians and how I carried you away on eagles' wings and brought you to me. So now, if you listen closely to my voice and keep my covenant, you will be my personal possession out of all the peoples; for the whole earth is mine. For me you will be a kingdom of priests and a holy nation.'"
>
> (Exodus 19:3-6a)

Once again, the initiative is clearly in the hands of God, who liberated the hearers and brought them to himself. But this God is a God who **speaks** — not a puppet-master who pulls strings but a communicator who seeks a relationship of reciprocity. Although everything begins with God's act, it cannot end there. So now, those who were liberated are offered a chance to enter consciously and willingly into the relationship; God invites them to listen to (the root meaning of "obey") his words and to accept the pact he offers. In so doing, this motley crowd of former slaves will become a people, God's own people.

It would be misleading to see this offer as a privilege, as if

God were choosing one part of humanity and rejecting the rest. The text clearly states that the whole earth belongs to God, and so any particular choice can only be understood in reference to this "whole" which is God's overriding concern. A key to this seeming paradox of universal concern and particular choice is found in the expression *a kingdom of priests and a holy nation*. In the ancient world, priests were people who mediated between the deity and humanity; if Israel receives the call to be a priestly nation, that is another way of saying that it serves as a channel to allow the living God to enter into the warp and woof of human history. To use a more comprehensible language, the covenant makes Israel a visible sign of God's presence in the world, a "burning bush" to attract others to an encounter with the Wellspring of all that exists. By choosing a people, God is kept from being confined to some inaccessible "heavenly" realm. The universe is shown to be sacramental, open to the eternal; the adventure of incarnation has begun.

According to the logic of the covenant, Israel is *a kingdom of priests* for two different but intimately related reasons. First of all, because of God's choice and call. Without this prior intervention of God, nothing is possible. The beginning can never be the work of human beings. No way exists that could cause them to decide of themselves to communicate something of the divine; it would be an intolerable pretension on their part. No exercises, training or reflection will ever make it possible. I do not find myself "called" or "chosen" as a result of something I have done myself; I simply become aware that the living God has already entered into my existence.

Still, we must immediately add that this divine choice or call does not abolish human activity or render it unnecessary; rather, it brings it fully into its own. Israel is called to *hear* and to *keep* God's words, in other words to live in such a way that their life is effectively a sign of God's identity and presence. Consequently, the covenant necessarily involves an invitation to those called to use their intelligence and energy to make choices so they can live in harmony with their deepest identity as God's people. It is this context that gives us a correct understanding of the dimension of "commandment" inherent in any relationship with God. This dimension is necessarily present not because God is some kind of tyrant jealous of human autonomy, but precisely for the opposite reason — because God takes human freedom seriously. God cannot make us "automatically" signs of his presence; all God can do is to appeal to our ability to understand the relationship he offers us and to act in conformity with that offer.

We can say the same thing starting from the notion of **freedom.** The prologue to the TEN WORDS presents us with a God who is essentially a Liberator, who calls people out of the house of servitude and therefore makes an existence in freedom possible. But what in fact does it mean to be free? As Israel will soon discover, it is not enough to leave behind the "house of servitude" to enjoy unhampered the benefits of a life of liberty. A reflection on the true meaning of freedom brings us to the heart of the significance of the TEN WORDS, and indeed the whole notion of divine law.

If we start with the concept of freedom as it is understood today, we shall see more clearly what is unique in the biblical outlook. For a good many of our contemporaries, being free means doing what I want, when I want. It is thus essentially rooted in the self, a self that has no other guide than itself and is set up over against all the other realities in the universe. Since in this way of seeing anything outside the self — other persons, material necessities, commitments — is a limitation of my free-dom, it follows that perfect freedom would mean being a universe unto myself, being "God," or more exactly a god who is misconceived as the perfectly self-centered being, the ultimate Self.

Biblical revelation offers us a quite different vision of freedom. For the Bible, freedom is not self-created. Far from being rooted in an autonomous self, it is a gift that comes through an encounter with the living and true God who calls me out of the house of servitude. And it involves discovering my identity as one among others, as part of a people. Freedom in the Bible is not individualistic; it flows from a shared life. In short, in this way of seeing, the other (both the great Other we call God, and our fellow human beings), far from being an obstacle to freedom, makes it possible; freedom is the consequence of a certain kind of **relationship.**

The God of the Bible brings human beings out of the house of servitude to allow them to enter the land of freedom. But the land of freedom is not merely another part of the earth, for example Palestine as opposed to Egypt, or the New World as opposed to Europe. Depending on the way we live — and the Bible is an eloquent witness to this — we are perfectly able to recreate an existence as slaves even while being comfortably settled in the Promised Land. In fact, rather than being merely a geographical reality, the land of freedom is defined by the words God addresses to the people that indicate their ongoing relationship to him, *the words of the Covenant*. It is this ongoing relationship that guarantees their freedom, and so the TEN WORDS in fact delineate **the boundaries of a space of freedom** or, to make the image more dynamic, they mark the road that leads to the fullness of liberty and happiness. They indicate the parameters that make possible a fully human life.

Considering the TEN WORDS as the parameters of a space of freedom helps us to understand why almost all of them are formulated in a negative fashion. Essentially they tell us what **not** to do, and people have sometimes used this fact to minimize their importance, contrasting the putatively negative, condemnatory morality of the Old Testament with the positive injunction to love that characterizes the Gospel of Jesus Christ. Rather than falling into such a facile opposition, it is essential to realize that the "negativity" of the TEN WORDS is an expression of their significance as **boundaries.** They do not attempt to control all of life, but merely to set the parameters that make freedom possible. It is then up to us to use our freedom, which practically speaking means our intelligence and our will, to create a life worth living within the space thus opened up. The commandments tell us when we have overstepped the bounds and are no longer in the space of freedom; they thus give us indirect indications as to what a fully human life might consist in. But as formulations they are incomplete — and intentionally so. By their very nature they leave room for the working out of our freedom and for the Spirit of God.

It is certainly not by chance that we find an identical logic in another of the foundational stories of the Hebrew Scriptures, the account of the first man and woman in chapter 2 of the Book of Genesis.

> The Lord God took Adam and settled him in the Garden of Eden to cultivate it and to take care of it. And the Lord God commanded Adam, "You are free to eat

of all the trees in the garden. But from the tree of the knowledge of good and evil you must not eat, because on the day you eat of it you will surely die."

(Genesis 2:15-17)

Here, the space of freedom is described as a beautiful garden which human beings are called upon to tend. In that garden they are *free to eat of all the trees*; God has no intention of controlling their every move and choice. On the contrary, God begins by encouraging them to use their freedom, for that is precisely what makes them human. And yet, we would not be in the real world unless these words of liberation were completed by a "negative commandment" that protects the liberty which has been offered. There is one tree whose fruit they must not eat, for in so doing they leave the space of freedom, shown graphically later on in the story by the exile from Paradise (Genesis 3:23-24). If we ask why there must be one tree that cannot be touched, why the space of freedom is not unlimited but of necessity comes up against a boundary, the answer is that this boundary represents the Other, the relationships that are essential to the exercise of freedom in the real world. Without the limit represented by the "forbidden fruit," we would be trapped forever in a solipsistic universe, unconscious prisoners of our own egos. Once again, the negative commandment bears witness to the fact that freedom is not egocentric; rather, the fullness of human life comes into its own in a network of relationships. The TEN WORDS have no other rationale than to situate the human being in that network of relationships which makes true life and happiness a real possibility.

In the language of Scripture, "eating from the tree of the knowledge of good and evil" (cf. Genesis 2:17) means arrogating to oneself the power to be the sole judge of one's behavior. Far from being a prohibition with a specific, limited content, God's words to Adam express the essence of the commandment as such — the call to take the Other's presence into account, to realize that I am not the Source. In this respect, it is the other, "negative" side of the Source. *The tree of the knowledge of good and evil* is the shadow of *the tree of life* (cf. Genesis 2:9).

There will not be other gods for you
before my face.

You will not make yourselves
a sculpted image,
nor any representation of that
which is in the heavens above
or which is in the earth below
or which is in the waters beneath the earth.

You will not bow down before them
and you will not serve them,
because I am the LORD your God,
a jealous God,
visiting the iniquity of the fathers on the sons,
on the third and fourth generations of those who hate me,
but showing faithful love to a thousand [generations]
to those who love me and keep my commands.

You will not misuse the Name of the
LORD your God,
because the LORD will not hold innocent
whoever misuses his Name.

(Exodus 20:3-7 / Deuteronomy 5:7-11)

Before examining in detail the rest of the TEN WORDS, we need to say something about the structure of the text. The tradition of the TEN WORDS is linked with their having been written on *two stone tablets* by God (Deuteronomy 5:22; cf. 4:13) or Moses (Exodus 34:28-29). This has led to various attempts to find a two-part structure in the text. Christian thinkers, going back at least to the fourth century (Saint Augustine), have used a Gospel passage as a basis for this division. Asked to name the greatest commandment in the entire Torah, Jesus mentioned two: to love God above all things and to love one's neighbor as oneself (Mark 12:28-34). The TEN WORDS can thus be conveniently divided into those concerning our relationship with God, and those concerning our relationship with our fellow human beings.

While such a division does capture an important aspect of the text, modern analyses have discerned a more complex structure, one in three parts. They note that the passage begins with God speaking in the first person about his relationship to human beings, and ends with WORDS dealing solely with human relationships, with no mention of God. Between these two poles, there are WORDS that bring together God and neighbor, speaking of God in the third person. This middle section is likewise carefully constructed, also in a threefold way: the center is surrounded by two WORDS; it begins with one that deals primarily with God, the saying about misusing the divine Name, and ends with another that deals primarily with humans, the saying about honoring one's parents. In the exact center of the text, we find the WORD concerning the Sabbath, which as we shall see is the focal point where God and humanity come together. This three-part interpretation does not in fact contradict the preceding two-part analysis but rather completes it, emphasizing that God and humanity are not simply set side-by-side. There is a movement in the text, a movement starting from God and going by stages towards human beings. If we are permitted to employ a later Christian category, we could call this a movement of incarnation.

Let us begin, then, with what some refer to as the first of the two tablets. After telling his people who he is and what he has done for them, God explains what their primary response must be. *There will not be other gods for you before my face.* Although the formulation is a bit ambiguous, the sense is clear: "You will have no other gods besides me, in addition to me."

It is important to emphasize that this WORD does not imply that no other gods **exist.** In fact, such an assumption robs the statement of much of its force. At that time, the presence of numerous deities in people's lives was taken for granted. Not only did each nation have its pantheon, its hierarchy of gods, but supernatural beings were found in all of life's varied dimensions. There was the goddess of the hunt, the tutelary deities of the household, the god of war, the god or goddess of this mountain or of that river, and so forth. In the religion of antiquity diversity goes without saying; what poses a problem is the unity between the different manifestations of the sacred.

So it is highly significant that, right from the outset, the TEN WORDS clearly distance themselves from the ordinary religious consciousness of the age. The space of freedom they delineate requires a clean break with a polymorphous religiosity. The God of the Bible accepts no rivals for his people's affection. As a following verse puts it, this God is a *jealous God.*

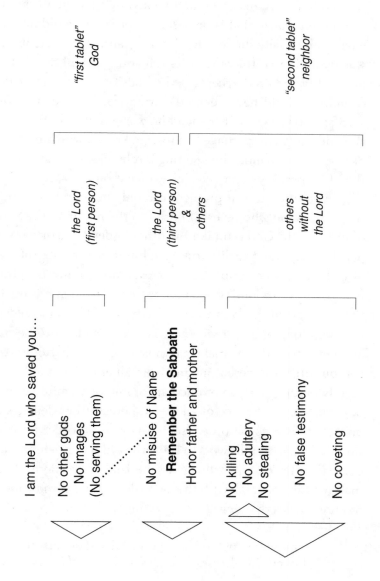

STRUCTURE OF TEN WORDS

I am the Lord who saved you...

No other gods
No images
(No serving them)

the Lord
(first person)

No misuse of Name
**Remember the Sabbath**
Honor father and mother

the Lord
(third person)
&
others

No killing
No adultery
No stealing

No false testimony

No coveting

others
without
the Lord

"first tablet"
God

"second tablet"
neighbor

Since for us the word *jealous* has overwhelmingly negative connotations, we may well be shocked by such an affirmation. We should realize that Israel's contemporaries would no doubt have been equally shocked by this new faith. The ancient world was by and large tolerant in its religious sensibilities; rules of hospitality required accepting the gods of one's host or one's friend. It would have seemed normal for a traveler to offer sacrifices to the gods of the land he was passing through, or for a maiden given in marriage to a foreign king to worship the gods of her new husband. The seeming intolerance of Israel's God is therefore perplexing; it calls for explanation.

A solution to this problem can only be found in the identity of the One who reveals himself to the nation as the Source of its life. This God is unlike any other, indeed of a different order than any other reality to which humans attribute the name of god. Were God simply the greatest among a host of spiritual beings, or even a kind of "first among equals," then it is obvious that such a deity's claim to exclusivity would be an intolerable presumption, an act of violence. For such a claim to be made authentically, the One making it must be not just better or stronger, but utterly different in kind from all else. This God cannot merely be the guardian of one part of life, of a limited domain, but must be the Source of all life. Whereas other deities shore up a particular social order (society) or world order (cosmos), this God calls his followers to leave the old order behind, to accompany him on a pilgrimage to the land of freedom. And to make possible a break with the old order, a total commitment is required, a yes that engages the whole personality.

 This notion of God is so powerful and original that Robert Sokolowski, *The God of Faith and Reason:*

*Foundations of Christian Theology* (University of Notre Dame Press, 1982) is able to summarize what is unique in the biblical outlook in a single phrase, called by him "the Christian distinction" namely, that God plus creation is not greater than God alone. See especially chapter 2, "Pagan Divinity."

The God of the Bible can thus ask human beings, without violating their integrity, to say a yes that is not on the same level as any other yes, that recapitulates the gift of their entire being. But if this is the case, it follows that there must be something in human beings able to gather together all the strands of their being and bring them to God. This possible locus of unity is what the Bible often calls the heart, referring by this not just to one human faculty among many but the underlying reality capable of hearing and responding to the divine call. Although it includes different aspects of human intelligence and will, in the final analysis the heart is the unity of the personality revealed when a person, in obedience to a call that comes from elsewhere, leaves the known world and sets out in trust toward a promised land as yet unknown.

Why is worship of this God different from that of all others? In the text of the TEN WORDS, there is a play on words that helps us to answer this question. We read that the God who *brought [us] out... from the house of **servitude*** commands us not to *bow down before or **serve** other gods*. Worshiping other gods is thus implicitly described as the return to a condition of servitude. Following God towards a land of freedom implies breaking the ties that bind us to other gods and to the social, political and cultural order they undergird, whereas allegiance to them would mean becoming slaves once more. To understand the significance of this theology for us today, we should not see these "other gods" in the first place as the divinities of the great world religions, but rather as realities much closer to us such as wealth, success, efficiency and power. These realities mobilize the energies of many of our contemporaries, by claiming to offer the fullness of life and happiness. As soon as they are taken as absolutes, however, they end up making us captives. When a part of the universe is mistaken for its Source, the human heart becomes trapped and slowly dies of thirst. The slaves take charge of the country and enslave their masters. What seemed at first to be a beautiful palace is finally revealed to be a prison, and even a tomb.

The *words of the covenant* thus begin with the revelation of the God who invites us to undertake a journey beyond the constraints and traps of a this-worldly existence, not because the world is evil in itself, but because the human heart is made for something greater. We find the same logic at work at the beginning of the Gospel of Jesus Christ, when the Master calls ordinary men to follow him, and they leave family, work and home to set out on an adventure of trust:

> While walking beside the Sea of Galilee Jesus saw Simon and Simon's brother Andrew casting their nets into the water; they were fishermen. And Jesus said to them, "Come after me and I will make you fishers of people." And at once they left their nets and followed him.
> (Mark 1:16-18)

Only a God who knows what is in the human heart (cf. John 2:25), because he created it, can motivate such a radical yes without its being an act of violence, but rather a revelation of our true identity and thus a gateway to freedom.

In the first table of the TEN WORDS, we find a development in three stages. First of all come verses 3 and 5a. God defines himself as the one without peer, who can thus make a unique claim on human allegiance. This global statement becomes more explicit in verse 4, the injunction against making images. Here, too, we find something which runs counter to the religious sensibilities of the age. In the ancient world, many nations represented the divinity by means of statues, usually depicting figures taken from the animal world such as a serpent, a bull, or sometimes even a human form. The God of Israel, on the contrary, refuses to be encapsulated in such an image. The significance of this prohibition involves at least two distinct aspects. First of all, if God is the Creator, the Source that cannot be confused with any reality accessible to human perception, then the attempt to symbolize him by a part of creation is fundamentally flawed. Here we return to the basic distinction between the God of the Bible and the gods of the nations, who are implicitly considered as subordinate to the cosmos as a whole. The impossibility of identifying Israel's Lord with any reality within the universe follows directly from the specific identity of this God.

Secondly, the pretension of human beings to *make* an image of God is equally mistaken. It implies a knowledge or expertise on their part that prevents God from exercising his sovereignty. The roles are subtly reversed. Instead of being the one whose ways are inscrutable, who leads us on a journey into the unknown towards a land of freedom and happiness, God is implicitly reduced to an object of human comprehension and control. The satire against the makers of idols in Isaiah 44, though it comes from a later age, makes this dynamic explicit: these images are nothing but a combination of created realities (*a block of wood*, Isaiah 44:19) and human labor, so those who accord importance to such things *are feeding on ashes* (Isaiah 44:20) and will awaken one day to find their hopes brutally dashed.

The human motivations behind the fabrication of an idol are shown with a great deal of psychological perspicacity in the account of the golden calf in chapter 32 of the Book of Exodus. Moses has gone to meet God on the mountain and has not yet returned; God remains invisible and seems to be absent. It is therefore not surprising that the Israelites, beset by fear and insecurity reinforced by the disappearance of their leader, demand a token of the divine presence able to be seen and touched, something they have at their disposition. Aaron agrees to their request, understandable in the context of the outlook of the age, and fashions the statue of a young bull out of precious metals.

The very way in which the story is constructed, however, shows the futility of such an attempt. The people ask for *a god to go before them* (Exodus 32:1), in other words a deity that will open the way towards the land of freedom and happiness. But it is obvious that a metal statue cannot accomplish this mission. For such a statue to move at all, those who made it must carry it on their shoulders. When human beings try to create a god in their own image, this god does not "go" anywhere at all. It cannot lead people to the fullness of life, since in the final analysis it is nothing but a projection of their own fears and hopes.

 Images play a significant role in some strands of the Christian tradition, and this has been a locus of controversy not just with Jews and Muslims, but within Christianity as well. In the West, the dispute was rekindled at the time of the Reformation, though in the Eastern Church it had already been dealt with exhaustively and profoundly at the time of the controversy over icons. Confronted with iconoclastic tendencies which considered the veneration of icons as the intrusion of a pagan mentality into the Church, the defenders of the orthodox faith maintained that things had changed fundamentally as a result of the incarnation of the Son of God. A brand-new situation came about when the divine entered into human history; in Jesus, *image* (eikôn) *of the invisible God* (Colossians 1:15), the Invisible took on visible form. Icons are copies of this visible form, not a human attempt to "fix" the transcendent Source: there are no legitimate icons of the Father, *who dwells in inaccessible light, whom no one has ever seen or can see* (1 Timothy 6:16). Painting, or rather "writing" an icon is an act of obedience to a God who has taken the initiative by revealing himself. It thus differs fundamentally from carving an idol; it is more akin to the behavior of a prophet's disciple writing down his master's oracles, or a scribe copying the Word of God on a parchment scroll. By sending his Son into the world, God reconciled the aspirations of humanity to "see God" with faith in a deity utterly beyond the created universe.

At this point in our reflection, it behooves us to say a word about the verses which define the activity of *the jealous God.*

I am the Lord your God, a jealous God, visiting the iniquity of the fathers on the sons, on the third and fourth generations of those who hate me, but showing faithful love to a thousand [generations] to those who love me and keep my commands.

(Exodus 20:5b-6; Deuteronomy 5:9b-10)

For a modern sensibility these words are practically incomprehensible, primarily because the notion of personal responsibility is for all intents and purposes absent in them. It is hard to imagine anyone today ascribing a moral responsibility to people for acts undertaken by their ancestors. In ancient Israel, however, the notion of personal responsibility would only become crucial at a later date, at the time of the prophets Jeremiah and Ezekiel around 600 BCE (Jeremiah 31:29-30; Ezekiel 14:12-20; 18:1-32; cf. Deuteronomy 24:16, 2 Kings 14:6). At this stage of the nation's self-consciousness, the accent is not on the individual man or woman but on the common life shared by all.

If we leave to one side the notion of **moral** responsibility, however, we discover that this text still has a lot to say to us. It provides a valuable corrective to contemporary Western society with its excessively individualistic ethos, by enunciating what we can call the **law of solidarity**. In this way of thinking, God has created a universe in which what we do has consequences not just for ourselves but also for others, in particular for those who come after us. Expressed this way, this law should not be alien to our experience. It is not hard for us to understand that families in which the parents have problems they have not dealt with themselves risk passing on these problems to their offspring in one way or another, whereas those who create a home life of acceptance, listening and understanding will more likely than not have children who behave in the same way later on in life. And this law does not only hold on an individual level. A nation that has undergone years of dictatorship or corruption cannot restore a healthy social fabric overnight, simply by removing the dishonest leaders. And as the ecological movement constantly reminds us, it is our children who will have to pay the price for our unbridled habits of consumption that are polluting the planet. In short, for good or for evil, our actions and choices affect the lives of untold others who follow in our footsteps.

Against the background of this fundamental law of solidarity that rules the universe, the text has something even more important to say. Wickedness casts its pall over three or four generations, whereas good has effects that last for thousands of generations, for ages untold. A simple contrast of numbers expresses a profound truth, namely, in God's universe, good and evil are not on the same level. Evil does indeed have its painful consequences, which even God cannot eliminate by magic; but when all is said and done, in comparison to the power of divine love they are like a drop of water in the ocean. Because of who the Creator is, the universe is biased towards the good. One of the psalms describes the same "good news" in a similar fashion:

> [God's] displeasure lasts only a moment;
> his goodwill is for a lifetime.
> Weeping may come to stay the night,
> but in the morning, shouts of joy. (Psalm 30:5)

The third and final stage of the biblical injunction to "let God be God" concerns the divine **Name**. This God is unique, cannot be captured in an image, and finally, even the divine Name must be treated with infinite respect. It is well known that in the Bible, as in most traditional civilizations, names are extremely significant. Never simply arbitrary labels, they participate in the reality of what they refer to; in modern terms, they express and even embody its identity. Revealing my name to others is thus an act that has important consequences. By so doing I place part of myself at their disposal; I make myself vulnerable. That is why, in societies where names have retained their power, people often have a series of names to be used depending on the degree of intimacy with others. One's true name is reserved for the circle of one's closest intimates.

The divine Name does not escape this logic. Simply put, God's Name is his self-revelation. The moment when God reveals his Name to someone is thus extremely important. And the name of a god shares in the power of that deity. Moses understood this well when, after encountering God in the burning bush and being called to go to Pharaoh to negotiate the people's freedom, he asked God to reveal his Name to him. He was asking in fact for a powerful weapon, something he could make use of in order to accomplish his mission. God acceded to his request, but not in the manner Moses had hoped. For the Name revealed by God, *'ehyeh 'asher 'ehyeh* ("I am who I am"; "I will be who I will be"; "I am who is...." Exodus 3:14), situates God beyond all human attempts at delimitation. God can never be possessed, controlled or used as a means to an end.

The WORD about misusing the divine Name makes this explicit. Originally it may have been directed specifically against magic formulas by which human beings attempted to achieve mastery over the world by manipulating a superhuman power for their own purposes. It may likewise have applied to false oaths that made use of divine authority to cover human wrongdoing. But in a wider sense, the WORD refers to all attempts to use God for our own ends. We can do this in a host of very subtle ways. Some people, for example, hardly ever think of God when things are going well, but suddenly find him indispensable as soon as a crisis arises. Probably without realizing it, they have thus turned the Creator of the universe into their own particular problem-solver. The God of the Bible, however, resists being exploited or manipulated in this way by every means possible, and does so not out of some perverse need to dominate or to remain in control, but because it is a question of his basic identity. Once again, far from existing in order to shore up a given human or natural world, God is precisely the One who calls us to leave that world behind in order to head towards a life we never dared hope for.

Discovering a further dimension of this WORD begins with the realization that God's people are those *called by his Name* (cf. Jeremiah 14:9). And as noted above, their mission is to be a sign of the divine presence at the heart of human history, to live in a way that reveals the identity of their God:

> The Lord will establish you as his holy people, as he swore on oath to do, if you observe the commands of the Lord your God and walk in his ways. Then all the peoples on earth will see that you are called by the Name of the Lord, and will be amazed at it.
>
> (Deuteronomy 28:9-10)

In living this way, the nation "glorifies or makes holy the Name of the Lord." When they do not live in accordance with their identity, though, they become a kind of living contradiction, and in biblical language, they "profane the Name of the Lord" (cf. Ezekiel 36:22-23). In a more extended sense, then, those called by God misuse his Name when their way of life is not in harmony with the faith they profess. That is why, at the beginning of the prayer Jesus taught his disciples, he tells them to pray that God's Name be made holy (Matthew 6:9). In other words, the Lord's Prayer asks that all may discover God's true identity through the lives of those who have been touched by him and who have set out on the road of discipleship. To the extent that they allow God to shine forth in their lives, they communicate his true Name to others.

Remember the Sabbath day
to make it holy.

Six days you will labor and do all your work,
but the seventh day is a Sabbath
for the LORD your God.
You will not do any work:
you and your son and your daughter,
your male and female servant,
and your animals and the foreigner
who is staying within your gates.

For in six days the LORD
made the heavens and the earth,
the sea and everything in them,
and he rested on the seventh day.

Therefore the LORD
blessed the seventh day
and made it holy.

(Exodus 20:8-11)

Observe the Sabbath day to make it holy,
as the LORD your God commanded you.

Six days you will labor and do all your work,
but the seventh day is a Sabbath
for the LORD your God.
You will not do any work:
you and your son and your daughter,
and your male and female servant,
and your ox and your ass,
and all your animals and the foreigner
who is staying within your gates,
in order that your male and female
servant may rest like you.

You will remember that you were a slave
in the land of Egypt,
and the LORD your God brought you out of there
with strong hand and outstretched arm.

Therefore the LORD your God
commanded you to make
the Sabbath day.

(Deuteronomy 5:12-15)

We have just examined the "first tablet" of the TEN WORDS, which defines a relationship with a God unlike any other — a God who admits of no rival, who refuses to be identified with any part of the universe, and whose very Name shares in his unique identity. As stated above, with the WORD about misusing God's Name we have entered the central or transitional part of the text. We are now beginning to move from the relationship with God taken in himself to God in the life of human society. This second section (Exodus 20:7-12 / Deuteronomy 5:11-16) refers to God in the third person, and comes between a first section referring to God in the first person, and a final section in which God is not explicitly mentioned at all.

We now come to the WORD which is found in the middle of this central section. It is also the longest of the ten. There is thus good reason to consider the saying regarding the Sabbath as the heart of the TEN WORDS. This circumstance, however, should give us pause. We have already identified a widespread tendency to find in the TEN WORDS a kind of natural or universal law, comprehensible and applicable to persons of good will in all times and places. Yet it is precisely this central WORD whose contingent quality is most striking. The week itself is a mysterious phenomenon, possessing no clear cosmological foundation like the day, the year or the month. And the fact that one of its days should be different from the rest has, on the face of it, no apparent justification.

Moreover, the more we examine this WORD, the more we are brought up short. First we are given a positive injunction, to *remember* or *observe* the seventh day of the week. When we ask what that means, we are simply told to abstain from work. From a biblical perspective, work refers to what human beings normally do, the reason for which God put them on the earth (cf. Genesis 2:15). So here all we are told is not to behave in our customary way; we are given no positive indications on how to spend the day. Then, if we ask why we must change our behavior on the Sabbath, we receive two radically different explanations. Here we have, incidentally, the one great discrepancy between the two versions of the TEN WORDS. In the Book of Exodus, the Sabbath is justified by the way God behaved in creating the universe: *on the seventh day [God] rested from all his work* (Genesis 2:2). Keeping the Sabbath thus means imitating God's own example, one might almost say being like God or, to use the language of the Book of Genesis, to be in God's image (cf. Genesis 1:27). The Book of Deuteronomy, for its part, relates the Sabbath to the act of liberation from servitude in Egypt. Although work is the natural condition of human beings, human sinfulness turns them into slaves and transforms meaningful labor, which is a sharing in God's creative activity, into harsh and unrewarding toil (cf. Genesis 3:17-19). By being freed periodically from work, then, Israel remembers that God called it from slavery to freedom; this freedom is explicitly recalled and celebrated at least once each week.

But beyond these specific justifications, the essential reason for keeping the Sabbath is because it is *holy*, in other words because it belongs to God. The days of the week are given to human beings for their use and enjoyment... but not all of them. God puts his mark even on the passage of time, retaining one day as his personal possession.

And this divine decision may in fact give us the key to grasping the meaning of the Sabbath. This "empty space" in the middle of our life, meaningless or at least enigmatic in human terms, is the footprint of God in the workaday world. It is an open space that communicates positive information, exactly like footprints in the sand, or like the empty tomb in the stories of Jesus' resurrection. Ceasing our habitual activity, since this has no obvious justification in itself, points to another dimension of existence. It tells us that the Source of our life is found not in what we do or even in what we are; there is a Reality beyond our world that gives meaning to it. Observing the Sabbath thus becomes a conscious way of putting into practice the first part of the TEN WORDS, of recognizing that unique Mystery we call God, whose absolute claim on our lives makes possible a truly human existence.

Life in a monastic community such as the one I belong to follows a similar logic. In Taizé, when the bells start ringing three times each day, everyone stops what they are doing, no matter how important or urgent this may be, and heads for the church to pray. It would not be misleading to say that, more than what we **do** when we reach the Church, it is the **fact** of going there that matters. By stopping periodically at more or less arbitrary times, we express the fact that at the center of our life there is the striving to make real a relationship with God, and that this gives meaning to all the rest. We can even bring this reflection a step further: at the very center of our prayer in Taizé, there is a time when we simply remain in silence for several minutes. If going to take part in worship is like entering a sanctuary or holy place, then this period of silence can be compared to the "holy of holies." We can do many things to express a relationship with that Other we call God, but we lose our bearings if we forget that, in the final analysis, prayer is not a human activity. So possibly the best way to guarantee the authenticity of our words, songs and gestures, is periodically to *be still and know that I am God* (Psalm 46:10).

Here we should emphasize that, while stopping our activity now and then can be a worthwhile practice in itself, particularly in a world that is growing ever more hectic and out of control, it is not quite the same thing as stopping in obedience to a WORD from God. A person who meditates daily for the purpose of quieting obsessive worries or of working more efficiently is doing something useful and beneficial, but in the final analysis is still living a self-centered existence. Only the reference to another dimension beyond the self, whether this dimension be explicitly named or not, enables us to break the yoke of slavery that binds us to the work of our hands. Once again, the biblical outlook tells us that we are unable to free ourselves, since we have no standpoint from which to do so. We can only receive liberty as a gift, by heeding a call that comes from beyond.

Is not the truth indicated by the WORD regarding the Sabbath more relevant than ever in our day? We live in a world where efficiency has become the watchword, where for most of our contemporaries life is so full that there is less and less time to reflect on what one is doing. One might be tempted to recycle the old metaphors of the rat-race or the treadmill, except that many of the things we do are — or at least appear to be — desirable: Where shall we spend our vacation this year? What film shall we rent this evening? Even entertainment and recreation have become a means to an end, taking the place accorded them by the all-encompassing logic of a highly rationalized consumer society. Life is filled with a host of possibilities, many of them appealing, and since we all want to stay in the running, there is simply no time to stop. But if we cannot stop, we will never have the distance necessary to choose, to discover if we really want to do all the things we are doing, if we truly wish to live the way we do. We will have become unable to hear the essential question any longer: is this what life is all about? Without realizing it, we will then have become slaves of the runaway world we have created.

But is there any alternative? Is it not easier just to give up the fight and make peace with this captivating if artificial world, seeing it as a kind of lesser evil? The answer to this question is not long in coming. In spite of everything, we are not the creators of this universe, and the day will infallibly arrive when that becomes evident. Eventually reality breaks in, our self-referential world falls apart and, whether we like it or not, we are forced to stop. With luck we may be able to postpone this encounter with reality to the day of our death, but is it preferable to wait until that moment to find out that we have never really lived? Far better to hear the call to stop that reaches us here and now in the midst of our hectic lives, that puts our human world in a wider and deeper perspective. *Be still, and know that I am God.*

Let us examine more closely now the justifications of the Sabbath in the two versions of the TEN WORDS. In the Book of Exodus, we are told to keep the Sabbath in imitation of God's own behavior. But how does God behave? Today, at any rate, almost nobody imagines that God required rest after the labor of creation. And even the Jewish rabbis of old distinguished between God's rest from the work of creating and his constant and necessary activity in sustaining the universe (cf. John 5:17). What meaning, then, can we find in this mention of divine rest?

Is the text not attempting to suggest that God has placed in the very structure of creation, symbolized by the week, a rhythm that enables it to point beyond itself? The universe as it comes from the hand of God is made up of work and leisure, giving and receiving, activity and passivity. No creature can keep going forever; there comes a moment when we need to stop. The truth of this may be borne in on us when some urgent task requires us to try and infringe this "law of nature." Perhaps we have to study night and day for an important exam, or finish a report that is long overdue. Or perhaps a rescue attempt following some catastrophe requires the rescuers to give their all. What happens? Try as we may, beyond a certain point we cannot keep up our activity. Simply put, we collapse. We need to be restored by sleeping and eating. This seemingly banal observation in fact reveals a profound truth. We are not the Source. In order to give, we must first receive. Thus already in the structure of the universe God has placed a reminder of our status as creatures, a call to stop periodically and return to the Wellspring of life. The Sabbath makes this structure explicit for believers; it is God's signature on the world he has created.

The New Testament goes even further in manifesting what is latent in this aspect of the creation story. With the revelation of a God who is Trinity, the rhythm of giving and receiving is found to be a constitutive dimension of the divinity. God is not only absolute Source ("the Father") but also the Son who can do *nothing by himself but only what he sees the Father doing* (John 5:19), who *lives because of the Father* (John 6:57). The mystery of God includes both Sender and Sent, Giver and Receiver, as well as a third dimension, the Sending or the Gift.

The theology of the Book of Deuteronomy presents in its turn another aspect of the Sabbath. It is a day given for the sons and daughters of Israel to remember that, thanks to the saving activity of God, they are no longer slaves but have received the gift of freedom. The Creator-God continues his work in history as the Redeemer. Stopping to call to mind their relationship with

God thus has important consequences for the self-understanding of God's people. Here we should recall the words found in both versions which emphasize that the Sabbath rest is not just for heads of households but also for all the inhabitants of the land, including even resident foreigners and beasts of burden. It is thus a day of fundamental equality, when everyone, from the king in his palace to the poor widow in her hovel, benefits from the same liberation. As God's day, the Sabbath is likewise, and consequently, a day when the nation becomes what it is called to be in truth — a people created by God to live in equality, justice and solidarity.

This second and equally important dimension of the Sabbath follows ineluctably from the first. The Sabbath is given as a reminder of what the "promised land" should have been but in fact never truly was; it offers a fleeting image of a society of equality and justice. Stopping to remember who God is, the nation by the very same act remembers who it is — a *people of priests*, called to be a sign of God's presence at the heart of the world. Awareness of this was never completely absent in Israel, but it is also true to say that from the beginning of its existence in the promised land, the nation was constantly in danger of forgetting the divine covenant which made it *a people apart* (Numbers 23:9); it tended to behave in a manner similar to all the other nations. The Sabbath thus also serves to remind the people of their unique identity as God's people.

This aspect of the Sabbath becomes even clearer when we examine, not the Sabbath of days, but the Sabbath of years. Every seventh year, in fact, Israel was called to cancel debts and set slaves free, so that *there be no poor among you* (Deuteronomy 15). The sabbatical year, and to an even greater degree the jubilee year, the Sabbath of Sabbaths coming after forty-nine years, was to be celebrated as a time to *proclaim liberty throughout the land to all its inhabitants* (Leviticus 25:10), a time of rest and celebration, a return to the roots which also served as an anticipation of God's future Reign in the midst of the present world.

With this as a background, we can better understand the attitude of Jesus towards the Sabbath. In Jesus' day the Sabbath was an important institution in Israel, and discussions of the correct way of observing it were common coin. It is thus not surprising that these discussions left their mark on the Gospels. At the same time, it is not always easy to understand Jesus' teaching regarding the Sabbath, especially since there is reason to think that even his disciples did not always see clearly what he was getting at. Things became even more complicated when, in the decades following his death, more and more of his followers came from Gentile backgrounds for which this quintessentially Jewish institution had little meaning. One could easily interpret some of Jesus' words and gestures regarding the Sabbath as a way of dismissing it out of hand, as if it were merely an irrelevant rite that distracted people from what really mattered.

Although this kind of interpretation is still current among some Christians (would not many understand a saying like Mark 2:27, *The Sabbath is made for human beings, not human beings for the Sabbath*, as a rather cavalier dismissal of its normative status?), deeper reflection should convince us of its inaccuracy. Whatever else he was, Jesus was a pious Jew, and no Jew of the first century of our era would deny the divine origin and the importance of the Sabbath. The simple fact that it is mentioned in both the creation story and in the TEN WORDS is enough to guarantee its centrality in the eyes of Judaism. In short, it is virtually impossible to maintain that Jesus could have rejected this key institution of the faith of his ancestors.

We are on much more solid ground when we realize that the central question in these controversies is not the importance of the Sabbath as such, but **what** it means and **how** it is to be observed. And behind these questions lies another, more fundamental one: "Just who is this God whose 'day' we are celebrating?" Here, we can readily expect to find a divergence between the outlook of Jesus and that of some of his contemporaries.

Let us look at one of these controversies, to understand more clearly what is at stake.

> Jesus went on from there and entered their synagogue. A man with a shriveled hand was there. And they questioned him, "Is it permitted to heal on the Sabbath?" They asked this in order to have a reason to accuse him. But he said to them, "Is there a person among you possessing a single sheep who, if that sheep were to fall into a pit on the Sabbath, would not take hold of it and lift it out? And yet how much more is a human being worth than a sheep! Therefore it is permitted to do good deeds on the Sabbath." Then he said to the man, "Stretch out your hand." He stretched it out and it was restored, just as healthy as the other one. Then the Pharisees went out and conferred about how they might get rid of him.     (Matthew 12:9-14)

At first glance, we appear to be witnessing a typical discussion among the Jews of those days concerning what kind of activity is lawful on the Sabbath. Upon closer examination, however, we can see that something else is going on. We are told that Jesus' adversaries asked the question because they were looking for *a reason to accuse him.* Their intentions are not transparent. Under the guise of trying to discover the truth through dialogue, they are in fact interested only in bringing down their "enemy" at all costs. At the end of the story, these hidden designs become manifest: *[They] went out and conferred about how they might get rid of him.*

Jesus, for his part, simply sees a man who is infirm, a being who does not possess the fullness of life. His primary interest is to restore that life, even if this brings him into conflict with those who have other priorities and eventually leads to his downfall.

Implicitly, then, the story asks us a question: "Who in fact is observing the Sabbath, Jesus or his opponents?" And this question has to be answered on two different levels. On the surface, the opponents of Jesus are moved by zeal for God's Law, whereas Jesus' concern is simply with the handicapped man. But on a deeper, more hidden level, the level of the "heart," the accusers are filled with hatred, jealousy and guile, while Jesus is motivated by love and special concern for the unfortunate. So who is keeping the Sabbath? It all depends on one's understanding of God. If God is essentially a lawgiver anxious above all that his commands, however arbitrary, be kept as punctiliously as possible, regardless of the deeper motivation for this, then Jesus' adversaries are right. If God is the Source of life who desires to communicate to creatures this life in fullness, then the Sabbath is fittingly observed where people's hearts are open to this life which comes from God and where they seek to pass it on to others. *It is permitted* (read: *God is glad for us*) *to do good deeds on the Sabbath.*

The story makes its point in a more subtle fashion as well. The man healed by Jesus is not just suffering from any ailment; he has a *shriveled hand.* And Luke's Gospel (6:6) even specifies that it is his **right** hand. The hand, and particularly for most people the right hand, is the part of the body used for working; in consequence, this individual is unable to do his work not just on the Sabbath, but throughout the week. If keeping the Sabbath is reduced simply to abstaining from labor, then, ironically, this man is particularly fortunate. No danger of sinning for him! The story thus implicitly shows where the logic of Jesus' opponents leads. It reveals the absurdity of a vision of life that would maintain that, in God's eyes, it is better to be paralyzed and not able to work at all than to be whole and risk profaning the Sabbath. This logic is in striking contrast to the outlook of Jesus himself, where God, life and love are united, especially on the day that belongs to God in a special way. Far from downplaying the Sabbath, Jesus shows its true significance.

The point of the narrative immediately before this one (Matthew 12:1-8), also dealing with the Sabbath, is more difficult to grasp. Jesus' disciples pick some grain to satisfy their hunger while walking through the fields on the Sabbath. When they are accused of breaking the Sabbath by some Pharisees, Jesus replies by quoting two examples, one from the life of King David and one concerning the priests in the Temple, where prescriptions are set aside because of something more important. The moral is apparently, "Here there is something greater than Israel's greatest king, and even greater than the Temple, where human beings come into contact with God" (cf. v. 6). We miss the point, however, if we imagine that Jesus is merely exalting himself according to some human scale of values. The "greater thing" is what Jesus and his disciples are doing at that moment: proclaiming that now God is finally fulfilling all his promises by coming into the world in a brand-new way in order to transform it radically. Greater than anything that took place in the past is the good news that something unique is happening **now**: *the King-*

*dom of God is at hand* (Mark 1:15). The Sabbath was given by God to be a sign of this Kingdom, an anticipation of a world where people are reconciled to God and therefore to one another. Jesus is making this reconciliation a reality here and now, and therefore his activity not only does not profane the Sabbath, but rather fulfills its reason for being.

Jesus' attitude towards the Sabbath explains why Christians gradually shifted the accent from the seventh day of the week to the "eighth day," in other words to the first day of a new week, the day of the Resurrection. Naturally this development was fostered when the followers of Jesus ceased to be primarily a group within Judaism, but instead formed communities where people of many different backgrounds shared a common faith. Christians of non-Jewish origin would not be expected to keep the Sabbath. But beyond this sociological evolution, a deeper truth is at work here. If Jesus, especially in his death and resurrection, fulfills the deepest significance of the Sabbath by indicating the imminent presence of God's Reign, then it is appropriate for his followers to celebrate the Day of the Lord first of all on the day of the Resurrection. We have seen that the Sabbath does not close the week but keeps it open, pointing beyond this present age to a time when God and humanity would live in perfect harmony. For Christians, this new world has already become a reality in Christ, specifically in his Resurrection, and so there is no contradiction between the seventh day and the eighth or first day properly understood. The latter "fills in the blanks," giving concrete content to what the former had expressed as a hope.

 "More than a 'replacement' for the Sabbath, therefore, Sunday is its fulfillment, and in a certain sense its extension and full expression in the ordered unfolding of the history of salvation, which reaches its culmination in Christ" (John Paul II, Apostolic Letter *Dies Domini*, May 31, 1998, § 59). The fact that, notwithstanding the Pope's remarks, many Christians have imagined that Sunday simply replaces Saturday for them, seems historically to have been due to an attempt to distinguish Christianity from Judaism, which naturally meant emphasizing the superiority of the former. Today, there is more and more widespread recognition that a "replacement theology" does not adequately conceptualize the relationship between Judaism and Christianity. This should also logically entail a reexamination of the relationship between Saturday and Sunday, perhaps seeing them as "two brother days" and meditating more deeply on the mystery of Holy Saturday in the Christian dispensation (*Dies Domini*, 23 and note 23). A way forward might be that of replacing an exclusive focus on Sunday with a celebration of a "weekly Easter triduum," beginning on Friday as a commemoration of Jesus' gift of his life on the cross, continuing on Saturday as the day of God's silence, a fulfillment lived in faith and hope but not yet definitively possessed (this would also be a day of solidarity with the Jewish people, an important dimension of whose vocation is to keep open the dimension of expectation and, on another level, with those who cannot believe), and culminating on Sunday with the explicit celebration of Christ's victory over the powers of death, which thus marks the beginning of a new week. In Taizé we celebrate such a "weekly Easter," with the prayer around the cross on Friday in solidarity with all who suffer across the world and a Saturday evening vigil of the light of Christ, concluding on Sunday morning with the festive celebration of the Eucharist.

Honor your father and your mother
so that you will have a long life
on the ground which the LORD your God
gave to you.

(Exodus 20:12)

Honor your father and your mother
as the LORD your God commanded you,
so that you will have a long life
and so that it may go well with you
on the ground which the LORD your God
gave to you.

(Deuteronomy 5:16)

When I was learning my catechism at the age of seven or eight, this commandment occupied the primordial place. It received a single, unambiguous interpretation; it was read (or misread) to say: **obey** your father and mother. The great sin for children at that time and place was disobedience — to parents first of all, and secondarily to teachers and other adult authority figures. In fact, such an interpretation of this WORD is not new; we already find it in the New Testament, in the **Haustafel** (rules for domestic order) sections of Paul's Letters to the Ephesians and the Colossians (Ephesians 6:1-3; Colossians 3:20). We should note, however, that immediately after telling children to listen to their parents the author turns to the parents, encouraging them to treat their children with gentleness and understanding. Already at that time, then, the WORD was implicitly seen to involve a certain reciprocity, and not apply uniquely to little children.

In fact, we can question whether it was ever meant primarily to refer to persons under age. Although the TEN WORDS are addressed to the nation as a whole (Exodus 19:25; Deuteronomy 5:3, 22), they are principally intended for fully responsible members, for adults and even more specifically heads of households. These are the ones who take upon themselves "the yoke of the Covenant" in the first place. Consequently, the injunction to honor one's parents would seem to apply first and foremost to the treatment of elderly people, ensuring that they not be forgotten or neglected by their descendants when they are no longer able to care for themselves. Treat the elderly with care and respect, this reading of the text seems to say, for they gave you life and made you what you are; one day you will be in the same situation as they are now.

A gospel text in which Jesus criticizes the Pharisees confirms this interpretation:

> And he said to them: "You hold on to your tradition and nullify God's commandment. For Moses said, 'Honor your father and your mother' and 'Anyone who insults father or mother should be put to death.' But you say, if someone declares to their father or mother, 'Whatever I would use to support you is korban,' in other words an offering to God, then you do not require them to do anything for their father and mother. In this way you use the tradition that was handed down to you to make God's word null and void." (Mark 7:9-13)

Apparently some people felt that they were fulfilling their duties by contributing part of their resources to the Temple, resources which otherwise would have been used to support their elderly parents. Jesus for his part condemns this attempt to use religion to excuse a lack of basic human solidarity. For our purposes, what is important here is that the WORD in question was seen as requiring adults to support their own parents who were nearing the end of their days.

We should perhaps stop and ask ourselves whether this interpretation of the command to honor one's father and mother is not particularly relevant in today's society. We live in a culture where "young is beautiful," where the rapid pace of change makes anything that is not new rapidly outdated. At the same time, thanks to improvements in hygiene, diet and medical care, people live longer on the average than ever before. Sometimes, their economic situation is quite precarious. In affluent societies, however, many of the elderly are taken care of materially, often in facilities created especially for this purpose. Once they can no longer keep up with the hectic rhythm of life in our day, however, they tend to be forgotten and left to an isolation peopled only by their memories, with death as the only thing to look forward to. The question deserves to be asked: by excluding the aged in this way, are we not only impairing their human dignity but impoverishing the rest of us as well, by eliminating from our lives a diversity that makes us all more fully human?

Leaving now to one side the question of to whom this WORD is primarily addressed, let us try to grasp its deeper meaning. The verb translated as "honor" comes from a root containing the notion of "weight" or "heaviness." We could thus express it as "to give weight to," to consider as important. What is the significance of considering my father and mother as important to my existence? It means that implicitly I realize that I am not my own source; I am not the author of my own life. The first tablet of the TEN WORDS is centered on belief in a God, the absolute and unique Origin of our existence, who calls us out of slavery to freedom. Recognizing this God means consenting to a change of perspective by which we recognize that everything is a gift, a gift that comes through a relationship with that mysterious Other. We are now asked to take a further step. Our life is indeed a gift from God, but this gift does not come to us from God directly; it comes through other persons, first and foremost our parents. The relationship with the absolute Source of life is mediated through relationships with our fellow human beings; indeed, the former creates the latter, since God saw at the beginning that *it is not good for humans to be alone* (Genesis 2:18).

Looked at in this way, father and mother stand for all those human relationships through which we receive from God what we need to be fully alive. Honoring them means recognizing my debt to my fellows, without whom I would not be who I am.

This very simple observation goes against something deeply rooted in our collective consciousness. Western society underwent its crisis of adolescence with the birth of modernism, when it strived to escape the tutelage of constituted religious and political authorities. Fully conscious of its own powers for the first time, it exalted the image of the "self-made man." I am not what an accident of birth has made me, but what I alone make of myself. While this outlook was undoubtedly comprehensible as a stage in humankind's coming to greater maturity, it is insufficient and even dangerous when made into an absolute. Today, as our world, especially in the West, heads into what some call a postmodern age, we are more aware of the impasses into which our exaggerated individualism and activism have brought us. It is nevertheless still not easy for many of us to realize to what extent our existence depends on interplay with the surrounding environment, especially the human environment. The heirs to the modern world need to realize that it is more accurate to say not "I am what I make of myself," but rather, "I am a unique person called to accept, develop and use the gifts I have received for the benefit of the human community to which I belong."

A further obstacle to understanding the WORD we are considering comes from the fact that we live in a society that is much more complex than that reflected in the Hebrew Scriptures. In ancient times almost everything came through the family, whereas in our world a host of institutions and individuals share in the task of formation. In the past, the first thing people received from father and mother was life itself. This is still true for us at present, though recent advances in the biomedical sciences may end up calling even this basic postulate into question, with incalculable consequences for the future of the human race.

Newborn children must also learn **how** to live, since human beings are distinguished from other species by the amount of information that is not programmed in them before birth but must be acquired by the organism: a human baby is born in a much more "unfinished" state than a camel or a dog. In ancient civilizations, transmitting this information was likewise primarily the work of the family, whereas today other institutions, among them schools, churches and the mass media, contribute to this process of education. In this context we touch upon the biblical notion of **wisdom,** which refers not to some kind of theoretical knowledge but attempts to answer the question "How can we live a life that is successful, in other words happy, fulfilling and useful?" Although in Israel of old there were professional teachers of wisdom, particularly at the time of the monarchy, the practical knowledge necessary for living was passed down from the old to the young, especially within the family:

> Listen, children, to a father's correction,
> and try and understand how to be intelligent.
> For I have given you good instruction;
> do not forsake my teaching.
> For I was a son to my father,
> pampered as my mother's only son.
> He taught me, saying:
> "Hold my words in your heart;
> keep my commands and you will live."
>
> (Proverbs 4:1-4)

53

The author explains that he is handing down in turn to his children, or pupils, what he himself once received from his own parents or teachers. Wisdom is thus essentially a **tradition,** which means something that is passed on or handed down (from the Latin word **tradere,** "to deliver up, to hand over"). The fact that in our day this word has been degraded to mean essentially "an outdated custom" reveals a great deal about the loss of our roots concomitant with the transition to modernity and the accelerated pace of change. Anything received from past generations, instead of being seen as a precious treasure to be conserved and passed on, is spontaneously felt to be irrelevant to the way we live our lives today.

In addition to life and instruction on how to live well, in the world of biblical times one's religious identity also came from one's parents. Judaism is still today a family-based religion: one is a member of the chosen people by virtue of being born into a Jewish family. And many of the practices of the faith were — and still are — learned within the family circle. We should note here that Christianity, by contrast, is **not** a family-based religion, despite the equation of the Christian faith and "family values" current in some circles. Although many of us received our faith in Jesus Christ from our parents, that is not at all necessary. On the contrary, the early Christians generally came to Christ in opposition to their background, and this still happens today with astonishing frequency. Perhaps this is why the figure of Abraham has always spoken so deeply to Christians, although not as the ancestor of a people from whom they are descended in a physical sense. What they can easily identify with is rather his departure from home in order to head into the unknown in the company of a pilgrim God (cf. Galatians 3:6-9; Romans 4).

And yet, although it does not necessarily come from our

biological parents, the Christian faith is also a tradition. Here too, the gift of God comes to us through other human beings. Even in the hypothetical and extreme case of a "Robinson Crusoe" who learns about Christ on a desert island after reading a Bible found in the sand, it remains true that the book he holds was translated and printed by someone. Moreover, before the invention of printing, generations of scribes had to have copied the text by hand. In short, there is no way to avoid the fact that a chain of real persons links the followers of Christ today directly to the apostles and to Jesus himself. A personal experience of Christ is of course essential; faith naturally moves from believing through the word of others to a more direct inner relationship (cf. John 4:42). Still, it can never be just an individual reality. By its very nature, faith creates communion between human beings and leads to the formation of a community. As *friends* of Jesus (John 15:14-15), we become friends of one another. Is not the Church in some sense a "society of friends"?

We can now ask the question, "How do we truly honor father and mother?" The answer can be found in another key passage of the Bible which, although not one of the TEN WORDS, has an almost equal importance. We first find this passage at the beginning, in the story of the creation of woman as a fitting companion to man:

> That is why a man leaves his father and mother and joins his wife, and they become one flesh.
>
> (Genesis 2:24)

We seem to be faced with a contradiction here. On the one hand we are told to honor father and mother, on the other it seems necessary to leave them. In fact, surprising as it may seem at first, the two texts form a unity. The underlying truth could even be stated more bluntly: the only way truly to honor those who gave us life is to "leave" them! To comprehend this somewhat provocative statement, we need to understand what this act of leaving entails. It clearly does not mean to abandon one's parents, to cut off all relationship with them, behavior which would indeed be in direct opposition to the letter and spirit of the WORD from Sinai. Nor does it even necessarily involve going off to live in a separate dwelling. The context of Genesis 2:24 is that of marriage. "Leaving father and mother" thus means leaving an old life behind in order to begin a new one. The old life was that of someone still immature, with no responsibilities; the new one is that of an adult, called to found a family of their own. And when we remember that at that time there was virtually no alternative to the married state, it is clear that "leaving father and mother" refers essentially to the passage from childhood to adulthood.

In other words, the best way we can show the importance of our parents for our life is to follow in their footsteps by becoming responsible adults in our turn who put into practice the best of what they have given us. The ideal presented here is not for us to remain dependent upon our father and mother for all of our days, but to develop the gifts received, passing them on in our turn to a new generation. We do not show honor above all by words, but by a way of life in which the seeds planted in us are brought to fruition.

In the Gospel, Jesus gives us an indirect confirmation of this link between honoring our parents and leaving them. Speaking to a wealthy man who comes to him in search of the key to acquiring eternal life, Jesus begins by telling him to observe the TEN WORDS, closing with the one about honoring father and mother. Taken out of its normal order in this way, it receives unexpected emphasis. When the man continues to insist that he wants to go further, Jesus invites him to sell all his possessions, to leave everything and follow him. And a moment later, he praises those who *have left home or brothers or sisters or mother or father or children or fields for me and the Gospel...* (Mark 10:29). There is therefore clearly no contradiction in Jesus' eyes between the two statements: by leaving his father and mother for Jesus' sake, the man would not have ceased to give honor to them.

It is true that many of Jesus' words regarding parents and family can seem harsh. To someone who wants to accomplish an act of respect towards his father, he replies, *"Let the dead bury their own dead"* (Luke 9:60). At another time, he apparently refuses to recognize his own family of origin (Matthew 12:46-50). He even goes so far as to say:

> If someone comes to me and does not hate father and mother and wife and children and brothers and sisters, yes, and even their own life, that person cannot be my disciple.
>
> (Luke 14:26)

 The use of the word "hate" here is a Semitism. The Semitic languages have difficulty in expressing comparisons, and tend to do so by using pairs of opposites. Where we would say, for example, "I like Michael better than Daniel" or "Mary is more beautiful than Elizabeth," in Hebrew or Aramaic one would say "I love Michael and hate Daniel" and "Mary is beautiful and Elizabeth is ugly." Since the above text also contains an implicit comparison, it should more accurately be translated "does not prefer me to his father, etc." Interestingly,

Matthew has interpreted the underlying Aramaic more correctly by translating: *Whoever loves father or mother more than me is not worthy of me* (Matthew 10:37).

Upon closer examination, though, we can understand that rather than rejecting the claims of one's family of origin, Jesus' words attempt to situate them within a more encompassing context which in fact gives them their true meaning — the claims of God. Ties of blood are not denied but are subordinated to a wider belonging: that of God's family, in which "hundreds" of brothers, sisters and mothers are joined in an intimate fellowship around the One referred to by Jesus as Abba (cf. Mark 10:30). It is not for nothing that the early Christians spontaneously used images of the family to express their new life in Christ. When they called each other "brother" and "sister," when the apostle described himself as the "father" or even the "mother" of those he evangelized (cf. 1 Thessalonians 2:7,11; 1 Corinthians 4:15; Galatians 4:19), these were far more than arbitrary metaphors. They expressed a new allegiance that cut across all the old human categories. The Gospel thus offers a way to "leave" father and mother unknown in the previous dispensation, possible now because Jesus has revealed and made accessible the universal dimensions of the family of God. Although some Christians express this new state of affairs by the radical sign of consenting not to have their own spouse and children, we should not forget that all followers of Christ are called in one way or another to witness to the unity of the human family, to show that the fundamental reality *is not Jew or Greek, slave or free, male and female, for [we] are all one in Christ Jesus* (Galatians 3:28).

This teaching of Jesus points in addition to the deepest meaning of parenthood itself. Up till now we have looked at this

WORD from the viewpoint of the children, but what does it say to fathers and mothers? Once again, if the WORD is addressed primarily to adults, then it speaks to people who are at one and the same time sons/daughters **and** fathers/mothers. And in fact, one of the essential meanings of the WORD is to remind us that, as part of the chain of generations, we all occupy both sides of the parent-child relationship, even though not always simultaneously. Even those who have no biological offspring of their own are somehow involved in passing on what they have received to those entrusted to them. So in listening to this saying about honoring their own parents, parents are invited to remember that they too are sons and daughters; they have received from others what they are now endeavoring to pass on in their turn.

By listening to this WORD, then, parents can avoid what is perhaps their greatest temptation: to mistake themselves for the Source. This temptation is particularly strong in our day, since we live in a world more and more subject to human control. In times past, it was naturally not unknown for parents to try and impose their own outlook upon their offspring. In some cases even, it went without saying that children would follow in their parents' footsteps. But families were larger, choices more restricted, the scope of human mastery more limited and, too, there was perhaps a greater unreflective faith in the spontaneous course of life. Today, for most of our contemporaries, a child is not a (perhaps unexpected) gift from God but the result of conscious calculation. Child-rearing is more and more seen as a human venture, the purpose of which is to reach the goals one has set in advance. In some cases, an economic model even predominates and children are implicitly seen as an "investment," whether material or spiritual, from which the parents expect a corresponding return. Today there is thus strong unconscious pressure to see a child as merely an extension of its parents' will. The natural human wish to want the best for those one loves is subtly perverted into the attempt to create another being in one's own image. And this cannot fail to have serious consequences for the life of the children. Although it is no easy matter to know that one's parents are indifferent or hostile, it is even more confusing to be the object of a love that is anything but disinterested. The natural impulse to develop one's own gifts and perceptions is nipped in the bud; any attempt to "be oneself" is felt as a betrayal and awakens intense guilt.

By remembering that they too had parents, therefore, fathers and mothers can vanquish within themselves the spirit of possession, the short-circuit by which they mistake themselves for the Origin. They will remember that they can only give to their sons and daughters what they themselves have received. In its own way, then, this WORD echoes the basic theme that we have seen running through all of the TEN WORDS up till now. God alone is the Source, and we are called to be reflections of this Source by first receiving what we then give. As Saint Paul put it in the Letter to the Ephesians: *I bend my knee to the Father, from whom all parenthood in heaven or on earth derives its name* (Ephesians 3:14-15). Human parenthood is by its nature derivative. One alone is Father in the full sense of the term (cf. Matthew 23:9).

In the Letter to the Ephesians, the author remarks that this is the first commandment linked to a promise (Ephesians 6:2-3). The promise is not, as is so often misread, *Honor your father and mother, that **they** may live long in the land...*, but rather... *that **you** may live long in the land*. In other words, the text implies that we will be treated by those who come after us in just the same way as we have treated those who came before us. When we are old and unable to take care of ourselves, we must turn for support to those whom we have prepared. They will act towards us according to the example we have given them by our behavior towards our own predecessors. Once again the TEN WORDS draw a picture of a world of solidarity, a society where no one is at the center but where all receive and give in turn, in a complex dance witnessed to among other things by the passage of generations. Thus does God's revealed Truth liberate us to act with true freedom in the world which we receive as a gift to be cherished and handed on.

*You will not kill.*

(Exodus 20:13 / Deuteronomy 5:17)

With these words, we enter the final section of the TEN WORDS, which concern our relationship with our fellows. Previously I noted that there has been a constant tendency in the course of the ages to claim that the TEN WORDS propose a "universal ethic" not limited to Jews and Christians. It is these final verses that could best justify such a claim, given the fact that in them the divine Name is not mentioned even once.

Nonetheless, were we to take this omission as an indication that belief in God is not required for a full and correct understanding of the text, we would be making a serious mistake. The question that needs to be asked is rather the following: why are these sayings, where God appears to be absent, placed precisely here, in a text that sets out the basic clauses of the covenant uniting the Lord and his people?

When the question is put in this way, it points to a deep and fundamental truth concerning the identity of the God of the Bible. Jesus expresses this truth when he links two apparently separate commandments concerning love of God and love of neighbor in answer to a question regarding the **single** greatest command (cf. Mark 12:28-34 and par.). In his first letter, Saint John makes the same point in an even more succinct manner:

> If God has loved us in this way, we too ought to love
> one another. (1 John 4:11)

We have heard these words so often that in general we do not notice a flaw in the surface logic that is in fact a key to their meaning. Logically the statement should read: "If God has so loved us, then we should love **God**." In the place where we should find God, however, we find "one another." A little later, John explains why this is so:

> If someone says "I love God" and hates his brother or sister, that person is a liar. For a person who does not love his brother or sister, whom he sees, cannot love God, whom he has never seen. (1 John 4:20)

In other words, the authentic touchstone of our relationship with God is the relationship we have with our fellow human beings, beginning with those with whom we are united by the bond of a common faith. This key teaching of the Bible is evident to us because of long familiarity; it has entered into the warp and woof of Western civilization. But seen from a wider perspective, the notion that our duties with regard to the deity are fulfilled by the way we behave toward our fellows is not a self-evident truth. It is rather a particular belief, a belief that flows from the specific identity of the God of the Bible that has been revealed to us.

This very same fundamental belief lies behind the "second table" of the TEN WORDS. God is not absent from them; rather, God is now accessible only through the relationship among human beings and, at the same time, God is fully accessible through this relationship. The commandments regarding our neighbors do not flow from strictly rational, humanistic grounds; they are an expression of the covenant with God. To wrong one's covenant partners is to wrong God. God sets himself as a guarantee of the order that makes a common life possible among human beings. This further implies that to understand the deepest meaning of these words, we cannot interpret them in an individualistic way. Although they are addressed to each person for his or her part (the verbs are singular, not plural), they are not principally concerned to determine behavior between isolated pairs of individuals but rather to define the good society, to tell us what makes freedom and happiness possible for all. They confront us with a choice: do we want a society based on violence, or one rooted in mutual solidarity? Violence versus solidarity: that is the alternative that appears in a host of guises as we look for ways of living together on this planet.

Having come this far, we are now able to grasp the meaning of a saying that Jesus considers so essential that he tells his disciples that it sums up all of God's teaching:

> Act towards others in exactly the same way you want them to act towards you; that is the Law and the Prophets. (Matthew 7:12)

To understand this "golden rule," we must see it too with reference to society as a whole. It defines a world of perfect reciprocity, in which no individual is at the center but all see themselves in function of a wider belonging. This is what the previous WORD tried to show in the specific case of the parent-child relationship, by telling us that none of us are merely parents or merely children. Looked at in a wider context, we are all both receivers and givers, with different accents according to the stages of life, and as we treat our parents so will our children treat us. Reciprocity of this sort is another name for solidarity, and according to the TEN WORDS true and lasting solidarity is only possible in the context of an all-encompassing relationship with the God who guarantees the quality of life among human beings.

God must thus protect certain realities to make possible a land of freedom and happiness for all. These realities are consequently not at our disposal, otherwise life together is undermined at its roots. What are these fundamental realities? That is what the next three WORDS attempt to define.

The first and most essential reality protected by God is **life**. The previous WORD already helped us understand that life is a gift, a gift that comes from God through the intermediary of other human beings. And now, we are explicitly enjoined not to destroy life. The Hebrew verb refers specifically to killing that is unlawful and willful, and thus the WORD could also be translated "You shall not murder." It does not explicitly address the issues of self-defense, war and capital punishment, which naturally does not invalidate later reflections on these questions in the light of the biblical message as a whole. In any event, the fundamental teaching of the Bible is that life belongs to God in a special way. Although human beings are called to welcome it, to care for it and to protect it, it is not something at their disposition, something over which they have dominion. In fact, it would be more accurate to say not that life is entrusted to us, but that we are entrusted to it. If we obey its promptings, it will lead us to God.

The world of the Bible is very concrete, and so instead of being defined in abstract terms, life is expressed by means of certain tangible realities, which are far from being mere hackneyed metaphors. The first of these realities is **breath.**

It was obvious to ancient people that one difference between the living and the dead is that the former have air moving in and out of their bodies. The word for "air in motion" can be variously translated as "breath," "wind," or "spirit" in our modern languages, but in the ancient tongues it is a single notion, which moreover has close affinities to the deity. When the second and older account of creation in the Book of Genesis describes the origins of humanity as the act of a God who blows the breath of life into the nostrils of a creature formed from clay (Genesis 2:7), there the gift of life is clearly linked to our kinship with God. Although we indeed belong to the earth, as is shown by the play on words between *adam* "humanity" and *adamah* "the soil," our horizon is much broader. Human beings have within themselves something which comes directly from their Creator and can never be reduced to a this-worldly dimension. Its home is with God, which explains why Psalm 104 can describe death as a kind of de-creation, a reverse movement in which the breath of life returns to God, leaving *adam* to sink back into *adamah*. Birth, on the other hand, is an ongoing act of creation:

> When you hide your face, they are terrified,
> when you take back your breath,
> they expire and return to the dust.
> When you send forth your breath, they are created
> and you renew the face of the earth.
>
> (Psalm 104:29-30)

A second reality that stands for life in the Bible is **blood**. This explains what may otherwise seem an inexplicable or even bizarre element of Jewish dietary prescriptions. Eating the flesh of animals is permitted, but the blood must not be consumed along with the meat:

> I will turn against any man of the house of Israel, as well as any foreigner living among you, who eats any blood, and I will cut him off from among the midst of his people. For the life of living creatures is in their blood, and I have given it to you to make atonement for your life on the altar, for blood atones by the life which is in it.... Any man of the house of Israel, as well as any foreigner who lives among you, who goes hunting and captures a wild animal or bird which can be eaten, must pour out the blood and cover it with dirt. For the life of all living creatures is their blood....
>
> (Leviticus 17:10-14)

When an animal was slain and offered as a sacrifice to God, the blood was supposed to be collected in a basin and poured out before the altar (Deuteronomy 12:27). This is an obvious sign, once we have understood the underlying symbolism, that life belongs to God and so must be given back to God at death. In this way of thinking, consuming the blood would be an attempt by human beings to go against the logic of creation and to appropriate the gift of life, turning it into something they possess and thus implicitly setting themselves up as the equals of God. In the text from the Book of Leviticus, moreover, the act of pouring out the blood is linked specifically to a rite of forgiveness, whereby the blood signifies the new and living bond created between God and his people that does away with the consequences of their unfaithfulness. The text goes on to say that even the blood of animals killed during a hunt must not be consumed but rather entrusted to the earth.

It is worth noting that according to these texts, not just human life but even the life of animals was seen as something sacred. One of the principal schools of thought that left its mark on the Hebrew Scriptures, the so-called priestly theology, reflected long and hard on these questions. According to this theology, God at first gives human beings and animals all the green plants for food (Genesis 1:29-30). In the original divine dispensation, humans were thus meant to be vegetarians. But God's original intention is soon disfigured by human wrongdoing, and so God is forced to make a new beginning, expressed in the story of Noah and the great flood. After the flood, the new beginning is described in these terms:

> Then God blessed Noah and his sons, saying to them: Be fruitful and multiply and fill the earth. You will be an object of fear and terror for all the wild animals on the earth and all the birds in the sky, for everything that creeps on the ground and all the fish in the sea. You have power over them. Everything that moves and lives will be food for you; I have given it all to you just like the green plants. But you must not eat meat with its life, in other words its blood. And of your blood, which is your life, I will require an account from every wild animal and from every human being; I will require an account of every human life from a person. Whoever sheds human blood will have his blood shed by a human, because humans were made in the image of God.　　(Genesis 9:1-6)

In this text, we notice some significant changes with respect to the earlier age. Now animals as well are given to human beings to eat, and this means that killing of a sort is explicitly authorized. It is as if God, recognizing that humans are presently not able to live up to the high standards originally intended for them, changes the rules as a concession to their weakness. The taking of life is henceforth not absolutely forbidden; it is merely limited. The act of not consuming the blood is now interpreted as a sign of respect for all life, replacing the original act of not killing. And human life comes under God's express protection, with an additional reason given to distinguish it from other living creatures: human beings are made in the image of God (cf. Genesis 1:27).

 The above development was studied extensively by Paul Beauchamp, "Création et fondation de la loi en Gn 1,1-2,4," in *La Création dans l'Orient ancien*, Lectio divina, 127 (Paris: Cerf, 1987), pp. 139-182.

An earlier theology had reflected for its part on the roots of human violence. The first murder mentioned in the Bible is found in the fourth chapter of the Book of Genesis, in the story of Cain and Abel, which follows immediately upon that of Adam and Eve. The message is clear: when human beings break their relationship with God, relationships between them no longer possess any ultimate safeguard. Already in the previous chapter, after not heeding the divine word, Adam and Eve saw their original unity degenerate into shame, accusation and disharmony (cf. Genesis 3:7, 12, 16). The story of Cain and Abel carries this logic to its extreme; brother kills brother out of envy and jealousy. And is not every murder in some sense a fratricide?

Two details in this story are particularly worthy of mention. After Cain has done his evil deed, God says to him:

What have you done? The voice of your brother's blood is crying out to me from the ground.

(Genesis 4:10)

These powerful words reinforce the symbolism of blood we have been examining. Life belongs to God and, when it is destroyed by human beings who take the law into their own hands, justice has been damaged and a situation created which calls for redress. By producing innocent victims, violence has a self-limiting effect, as it were, exerting a kind of pressure upon God to restore a just world-order. This aspect of biblical thought, so profound and far-reaching, is made difficult for us to understand because it was not always adequately distinguished from the notion of revenge. Often, in fact, translators use the word "vengeance" to describe this call for justice by the victims of injustice. But revenge or vengeance is in fact a caricature of the attitude we are attempting to describe. These concepts place the accent on the resentment of the victims and their desire to see the oppressors suffer in their turn, whereas the "cry of blood" is in essence a call for justice, aiming above all at the restoration of right relationships that have been destroyed by an act of violence.

 The history of the vocabulary in this domain is an eloquent witness to the complexity of the question, which touches deep chords within human beings. The words "vengeance, revenge" come via French from the Latin verb **vindicare**, a legal term the first meaning of which is "to lay legal claim to." It comes in turn from the noun **vindex,** another legal term referring to the claimant or protector who takes the place of the person wronged before the tribunal. This word seems to be made up of **vis,** "force, violence" and from the root of **dicere,** "to speak." The **vindex** in effect speaks to the judge about the violence done to his client. Originally, then, as is reflected in the English verb "to vindicate," it referred to the efforts of someone wronged to have his or her rights recognized by a superior instance and to receive compensation from the other party. The figure of the **vindex** thus has affinities with the biblical **go'el,** the redeemer or vindicator, and linguistically is comparable to the notion of the "cry of blood." The semantic shift by which "vindication" became "vengeance" is worthy of note.

The English word "vindication" is thus possibly the best word to express the goal of the "cry of blood," although it perhaps focuses a bit too narrowly on the condition of the victim. We must not forget that the restoration of justice inevitably changes things for the perpetrator of the crime as well. The word "justification" would also be a good choice were it understood in its original sense. Saint Paul uses it in his Letter to the Romans to describe the consequences of Jesus' mission. By his death and resurrection Christ "justifies" us; he restores justice, right relationships, by bringing us back into an authentic communion with God (cf. Romans 3:24; 4:24-25; 5:1, etc.).

 This is likewise the original meaning of "judgment" (**mishpat**) in the Hebrew Scriptures. The notion of **mishpat** refers primarily to the act of an authority (the elders, the king, God) which restores justice to a situation which had been thrown out of balance by evil actions. From the point of view of the victim, it is therefore synonymous with being delivered. To be judged is to be saved, vindicated, justified. In this outlook, the condemnation of the evildoer is at best a corollary, important only insofar as it returns things to the way they should be. Cf. Psalm 43:1: *Judge me, O God, defend my cause against an unfaithful people; from the deceitful and wicked deliver me.*

In fact, a correct understanding of blood-symbolism is crucial for understanding the many New Testament passages where the image is used to describe the mission of Jesus Christ. The Letter to the Hebrews tells us that the blood of Jesus *speaks better than the blood of Abel* (Hebrews 12:24), in other words, his life given for us restores truly and completely a right relationship with God, fulfilling the aspiration of all the innocent victims of injustice throughout history. This notion is expressed most dramatically in the Book of Revelation, in the vision of the scroll sealed with seven seals and opened by the Lamb:

And when he opened the fifth seal, I saw under the altar the souls of those who had been slaughtered because of the Word of God and the testimony that they gave. And they cried out in a loud voice, "How long, O holy and true Ruler, will you wait before bringing justice and avenging our blood on the inhabitants of the earth?" And they were each given a white garment, and told to be patient a little while longer, until the number of their fellow-servants and brethren who were going to be put to death like them was complete. (Revelation 6:9-11)

This text is often applied to Christian martyrs, or else to the martyrs of the Old Testament. It would be better, however, to see it as an evocation of *all the innocent blood shed upon the earth, beginning with the blood of Abel the just* (Matthew 23:35), *the blood of prophets and saints and all who have been slaughtered on the earth* (Revelation 18:24). The vision thus contains a truly earth-shattering message; it tells us that the spilled blood of the innocent is the true motive-force of human history. What "brings God down to earth" to rectify our errors and selfishness is not great deeds of prowess, whether intellectual or moral, accomplished by the best and the brightest, but the cry of innocent victims. Their seeming defeat is in fact the prelude to a more complete victory. It sets in motion a movement of deliverance that comes to a climax on the cross of Christ. That is what the opening of the next seal testifies to. The Hebrew Scriptures sometimes refer to the reaction of God's holiness and goodness in the face of sin, for the purpose of restoring a just order, as "the wrath of God." In the Book of Revelation, *the day of the wrath of the Lamb* (Revelation 6:17) is nothing other than the act of Jesus taking upon himself all human evil and suffering its consequences in his own body.

> When abused he did not abuse in return; he suffered
> but made no threats, placing his trust in the One who
> judges justly. He bore our sins in his body on the cross,
> so that dead to sins we might live in a right relation-
> ship to God. By his wounds you have been healed.
>
> (1 Peter 2:23-24)

By giving his life to the very end, Jesus both shares the fate of all the earth's victims and martyrs and ensures that their sacrifice was not in vain. He brings their suffering into his relationship with the one he calls "Abba" and, since the Father always hears him (John 11:42), we have the guarantee that this suffering is not meaningless. It leads to the disappearance of the old world-order marked by injustice and to the appearance of *new heavens and a new earth... where justice dwells* (2 Peter 3:13).

The mention of blood in the context of Jesus' passion also emphasizes the fact that it is not his **death** that has value in itself but rather the total gift of his life. God *takes no pleasure in the death of anyone* (Ezekiel 18:32), least of all in the death of his beloved Son. The fact that Christian teachers have not always clearly distinguished between suffering and death as the destruction of life, and these same realities as expressing the will not to cling to God's gift but to give it back to God by giving it for others, has in many cases fostered a morbid fascination with suffering and a denial of life, with the inevitable reaction of causing others to turn away from the faith. In concrete situations this can admittedly be a fine line to draw, since we cannot make a hard and fast distinction between submitting to an act of violence and consenting to a self-surrender in trust. It is nonetheless essential to remember that we are saved by Jesus' **blood,** in other words the free and voluntary gift of his life poured out for our sake so that it becomes for us a source of new life.

There is another aspect of the story of Cain and Abel that has a profound significance: in it we encounter for the first time the notion of **the spiral of violence.** After his crime Cain says to God, *"Today you are driving me from the land, and I will be hidden from your presence. I will be a restless wanderer on the earth, and whoever finds me will kill me"* (Genesis 4:14). Leaving the land of freedom, that space which is under the divine protection, means becoming an outlaw. With no God-given law to define and regulate human behavior, the "law of the jungle" takes over, the struggle of all against all, with the strongest conquering until they themselves are toppled in turn by a stronger newcomer. But even in this new situation God attempts to bring a modicum of order, placing on Cain a mark of divine protection (Genesis 4:15). This detail of the story confirms our basic claim in these pages, that God's Word or Law, far from being an obstacle to human fulfillment, makes possible an authentically human existence. The spiral of violence is merely one name for life which is out of control, unable to follow its true dynamism, turned in upon itself in an orgy of self-destruction. Only an act of liberation coming from Another, accompanied by words that explain it and give it a fully human dimension by asking for an intentional response, can transform the false freedom of anarchy into the true freedom of life shared in harmony.

You *will* not commit *adultery.*

(Exodus 20:14 / Deuteronomy 5:18)

After **life**, the next thing protected by God is the couple, or more precisely the family. Given the fact that in the first pages of the Bible, the couple man-woman stands for the fundamental human relationship that recapitulates them all (*"It is not good for humans to be alone,"* Genesis 2:18), we can say that in a wider sense, this WORD protects all forms of human relationship. And this is logical for, after life itself, what matters most is life with others. Human beings are not created to be solitary individuals; without the different forms of interaction that characterize our existence on this planet, no human life worthy of the name is possible.

To understand this WORD regarding marriage and the family, we must turn once again to the saying that goes back to the beginning of the Bible and that we looked at in the context of the relationship with father and mother.

> That is why a man leaves his father and mother and joins his wife, and they become one flesh.
>
> (Genesis 2:24)

What interests us now is the second part of the phrase. It says that the purpose of leaving father and mother is to join with another human being and become *one flesh* with him or her. This Hebrew expression does not refer primarily to sexual intercourse, as a modern sensibility might imagine. A more faithful translation would be: "… and they become one (new) human reality." Beyond the physical expression of this new oneness, the words *one flesh* denote the oneness itself — the constitution of a new family unit. The text thus points to something truly mind-boggling, once we have achieved the necessary distance to contemplate it properly: the roots of a new family are not biological, but human. In other words, a family does not come into being simply because human beings are capable of procreating offspring; ducks, dogs and even frogs can do that just as efficiently, if not more so. What constitutes a family is, rather, a human act, which the text from Genesis refers to as "leaving" and "joining," and which can be variously described using words such as "choice," "promise" or "commitment." God uses the act by which two human beings make a conscious and free choice, a promise to commit themselves to one another for good, in order to create the matrix for the origin and development of new human life.

Let us stop a moment and try to see just how amazing this is. In examining the WORD about honoring father and mother, we saw that all of us receive life from God through others. Our existence is not an absolute beginning; all of us are born into an already existing human world. There is a "given" that makes us who we are, a starting-point for our development as persons. We can and indeed must modify what we have received, making use of it in different ways, but we cannot deny it or escape its influence. Now this "given world," which appears to a child as immutable as the stars in the sky and the hills on the horizon, is in fact the result of human choices! Even our biological family is only "biological" in a secondary sense; it is first of all human.

This is shown most clearly in the case of a true marriage. God uses the life-commitment of two people to create a new human reality, which becomes a "given world" for other persons still to be born. This means that human beings are not only co-creators with God because they are able to conceive and bear life physically, although this is already a great miracle. They are co-creators because God endows certain choices they make with the power to determine the life of those they give birth to, to create the matrix for the development of their children as persons. It is thus fitting that, after life itself, God protects the bonds that unite human beings in a stable and ongoing relationship that leads to the birth and growth of other human persons.

This context provides us with a key to understand the teaching of Jesus regarding divorce. As in other domains, he elucidates fully what was already implicit in the TEN WORDS and the tradition of his people set down in the Scriptures. If, in order to make possible the creation of a new human reality, God commits himself alongside human beings who give themselves in marriage, then an irrevocable step has been taken. God's creative act cannot be undone by the vagaries of human behavior. *They are no longer two but one flesh. So human beings are not to separate what God has joined together* (Matthew 19:6). To clarify the underlying meaning, we should almost translate: human beings **cannot** separate.... Here as always, ethics follows ontology: it is folly for human beings to imagine they can undo the work of the Creator. When they attempt to do so, they leave behind the real world for an unreal world of their own making. If the dissolution of the marriage bond has been tolerated at certain times and places as a concession to human limits, this state of affairs nonetheless does not reflect the true significance of this commitment in God's eyes.

It is no secret that of all the TEN WORDS, this is the one most difficult for us to hear today. This is due to a host of factors. The rapid pace of technological advance has eroded traditional bonds and values. Immense new possibilities offer themselves to human beings, with the result that relationships have become much more fragile, having lost their socio-cultural moorings in a world that resembles more and more a planetary marketplace. The gradual, inexorable separation of sexuality and procreation calls into question the very notion of marriage as normative. An individualistic and self-centered understanding of freedom makes a lifelong commitment seem an intolerable captivity. For these and a host of other reasons, the traditional teaching in this area appears irrelevant to many today, whether they rejoice in the new ethos of liberation or look back with nostalgia and regret to a bygone era when things seemed much simpler.

 This growing rift between sex and procreation deserves to be examined more closely in order to reveal what is truly at stake here, beyond the old disputes, unfortunately too narrowly framed, regarding "the ends of marriage" or "acceptable means of birth control." In the final analysis, through our sexuality we are in communication on a bodily level with the wellsprings of life and creation. In traditional societies, notably in the Bible (see the previous chapter), everything connected to the mystery of life is **sacred** and therefore of the utmost significance. When sex is imaginarily removed from its true place in the scheme of things, it cannot but be trivialized. This leads sooner or later, by a kind of ricochet effect, to the loss of significance of life itself, henceforth reduced from an end to a mere means subject to different forms of manipulation.

What way forward lies open to us? First of all, it is useless to deny that we are indeed in a new cultural context which makes it necessary to hear the WORD concerning adultery in a new way. When Christians simply reaffirm the old prohibitions with a crusading zeal that may well conceal self-doubt and a secret apprehension, they unwittingly widen the gap between themselves and contemporary society. The Church is then seen as either irrelevant to life today or, worse, as an adversary of human fulfillment. Once again, the problem is not fundamentally ethical but anthropological and ontological. In other words, the question is not first of all "What should we do?" but "Who are we as human beings? What is human existence all about?" The answer to these latter questions promoted by large sectors of contemporary society leads to certain forms of behavior which may or may not satisfy those who practice them. If believers in the God of the Jewish and Christian Scriptures live in a different way from those around them, it is their responsibility to understand and explain why this way of life corresponds to an authentic vision of what it means to be human. They are asked *always [to be] ready to give answer to those who ask about the reasons for the hope which is in [them]* (1 Peter 3:15). In this sense, the breakdown of patterns of behavior that determined our lives in the past can be a positive opportunity, because it forces us to reflect consciously on the meaning of our existence. Notably, such a crisis of values requires us to grasp what lies at the root of every truly human relationship, not just that of the couple. If the essence of a relationship, expressed most simply, is a continuity of being-together over time, it follows that without an intention to consent to this continuity, we cannot speak of a relationship at all. I must have a reasonable expectation that the other person will be there for me tomorrow in a manner that is in continuity with the way he or she was there yesterday and today. This assent to continuity over time is what we call a **commitment** or a **promise**. By promising or committing myself, I give away something that I cannot take back, since it no longer belongs to me; I do something I cannot undo. This is not to say that commitments cannot change, evolve, become stronger or weaker, or that every form of commitment binds us irrevocably to another for life. It simply means that for a relationship to be human a dimension of fidelity is required — we expect people to behave towards us in line with their behavior in the past. And this continuity of behavior is rooted in a continuity in the realm of personal being: we can count on them to be there for us in the future in a way coherent with their presence in the past. We need to believe that, despite the inevitable vicissitudes of personal and collective history, they remain the same on the level of their essential being-in-relation. Without this faithfulness no trust in others is possible, and therefore no human society worthy of the name can exist.

Here we touch again upon the reality indicated by the biblical notion of the **name**. To be a person means to have a name. This name, given by others, establishes and represents an identity over time. By my name I am registered in the book of generations; henceforth I am set in a context that allows me to be the unique person that I am. Understood and employed correctly, my name does not imprison or trap me in an unchanging mold, freezing my creativity and condemning me to immobility. Rather, it expresses a core around which I can use my freedom to grow and relate to others. By situating me in the interpersonal world, my name frees me from being locked up in myself, subject to the constantly changing flux of my inner states.

A world without commitment and faithfulness is a subhuman or inhuman world. Indeed, it is not a world at all, because a world implies meanings shared in common. Such an existence without roots in a common soil would require me to reinvent my own world each day anew. Living without placing my trust in other human beings, I would be obliged to calculate at every moment how far I could go. It would be like trying to play a game whose rules are constantly changing and the alliances between the (nameless) players constantly shifting.

Does this describe the plight of at least some people today? In any case, the WORD concerning adultery offers a radically different vision of human life than one which sees freedom as the absence of all ties. In protecting the yes of a lifetime commitment in marriage, God guarantees the stability of all human relationships. God endows human beings with the power to give their word, and this word given and received creates something new. In this way trust springs up among us, and mutual trust makes possible life together with our fellows. Following the logic of the TEN WORDS, the gift of life leads inexorably to a life shared in common, from which new life can then arise and be nurtured. True freedom is lived out in a network of relationships consciously assumed and able to grow and evolve over time.

You will not steal.

(Exodus 20:15 / Deuteronomy 5:19)

This third WORD in the series invokes divine protection against violence which does not go to the point of taking a life. Some Bible scholars, returning to an ancient tradition, prefer to understand it as saying "You shall not kidnap." In their eyes, it referred originally to a greater crime than the mere taking of possessions, namely abducting people in order to sell them into slavery (cf. Exodus 21:16). This interpretation would maintain that after life and human relationships, it is the freedom to dispose of one's own existence that is a paramount good protected by God.

The mainstream tradition, however, has understood this WORD as referring to the theft of possessions, and here too we can find ample justification in the logic of the text. After life itself, and relationships among human beings culminating in marriage and the family, the TEN WORDS now turn to the relationship between human beings and the material world. God safeguards the link between humans and the infrahuman substrate of their existence.

This WORD has a profound anthropological significance, for it reminds us that we are not angels or ghosts. We are incarnate spirits, the point of junction where the spiritual and the physical world come together. The Greek philosophers spoke of man as a ζωον λογικον (*zōon logikon*), which we can loosely translate as "rational animal." The biblical view, although somewhat different, proclaims in its own way the composite or intermediate nature of man. We see this clearly in the second account of creation in the Book of Genesis:

The Lord God formed the earthling (*adam*) from the dust of the earth (*adamah*) and blew into his nostrils the breath of life, and the earthling became a living being. (Genesis 2:7)

Human beings are taken from the earth, more specifically the ground, the soil, and yet they have something else in them, a spark of life that comes directly from the Creator. They are at home on the earth, and yet not quite at home. One way in which this second dimension is expressed is by a longing that can never be completely satisfied by the good things of this world, a nostalgia perhaps expressed best by Saint Augustine at the beginning of his spiritual autobiography: "You have made us for yourself, O Lord, and our hearts are restless until they rest in you" (*Confessions* 1,1).

The WORD we are looking at, though, reminds us forcefully of the other aspect of human nature, recapitulated in the equation *adam-adamah*. We are not pure spirits but rather incarnate beings, and so a relationship with physical things is necessary for us to be fully ourselves. Here it is worth emphasizing that the Bible, as distinct from many other philosophies and forms of spirituality, including the Greek outlook mentioned above, in no way disdains the material side of life. In some worldviews the spiritual is good and the material is evil; the highest good to which human beings can attain is to cut their ties with the material world and live a purely spiritual existence. This only comes about fully at death, but it can be anticipated to a certain degree in this life by ascetical practices, by means of which one tries to detach oneself as far as possible from the corrupting effect of matter. The authentic Judeo-Christian outlook has very little in common with this vision of the human journey. The first chapter of Genesis shows us a God who is the creator of all things, visible and invisible, and tells us that *God saw all he had made, and indeed* it *was very good* (Genesis 1:31). All things created by a good God are good in their way. Evil does not proceed from matter but from a confusion of priorities, a misuse of created being by treating as absolute what is only relative. It cannot be emphasized too strongly that for the Bible, the physical or material dimension of life is incapable of corrupting by itself, for *to the pure all things are pure* (Titus 1:15).

We may imagine that a vision of reality which denies the importance of the material world is only of historical interest, a relic of a bygone age. In fact, the situation is more complex. Apart from minorities who explicitly follow a world-denying spirituality or philosophy, our affluent societies, where unbridled consumption reigns, witness in their own way to contempt for the good things of the earth. Such an outlook considers material things only as objects to be used and enjoyed, and not as the companions of human beings on their pilgrimage through time. This contempt is aggravated by the great development and expansion of the means of communication in recent times; people today live more and more in a "virtual" world, a world that in the final analysis exists only in their heads. The inexorable destruction of our natural environment, against which the ecological movement has warned us for so long, is simply a consequence of this inability to discern the true value of things. It is, in a certain sense, a form of theft. Here we are worlds away from the unified vision of the cosmos expressed so well in Saint Francis of Assisi's "Canticle of the Creatures," and in danger of falling into a new Manichaeism.

The WORD about stealing invites us to attribute true value to the material world by not making it a simple object of our appetites. At the same time, it defends the right of human beings to a full life, which necessarily involves a close relationship with material things. This is first of all true on the level of purely physical survival. Humans need food, shelter and clothing in order to continue to exist, and to deprive them of these things is thus an indirect but efficacious form of murder. We should not, however, reduce the impact of this teaching merely to assuring survival. Since we are incarnate beings, material things contribute to the working out of our identity, and it is this truth that forms the basis of the right to have possessions. Who does not have cherished objects, often of little value to anyone else, that help to define who they are? Such an object may be a well-worn article of clothing, an old book, photograph or recording, the loss of which would make us feel that a part of ourselves had been amputated. Indeed, for all practical purposes such things are an extension of our bodies. And bodies are not just something we **have**, but something we **are**. This WORD thus defines a human being as part and parcel of the universe, bound to the material world by indissoluble bonds. It is not for nothing that the prophets of Israel never saw salvation as a disincarnate state, situating it in some immaterial heaven; they longed rather for the transfiguration of the world as we know it into a world of *shalom*, of harmony and prosperity, a paradise where creation is not annihilated but reconciled:

> Wolves will dwell with lambs
> and leopards lie down with kids.
> Calves and young lions will feed together;
> a little child will herd them.
> Cows and bears will graze together;
> their offspring will rest on the same spot.

Lions will eat straw like cows.
Infants will play on the cobra's den
and babies reach out their hands on the serpent's lair.
No harm, no ruin
on all my holy mountain,
for the land will be filled with knowledge of the Lord
as the waters fill the sea.     (Isaiah 11:6-9)

The New Testament continues along these lines, speaking of *new heavens and a new earth, where justice is at home* (2 Peter 3:13). And of course, the deepest expression of this outlook is found in the doctrine of the resurrection of the body: the material universe, represented by our bodies, is not detrimental or even irrelevant. It is not left behind but transfigured in order to enter into an eternal communion with God.

In trying to understand the significance of the WORD against stealing, it is important not to fall into the trap of seeing it as an unlimited justification of the right to private property. Such an ideological understanding of the prohibition against theft has often been a temptation, generally as a cover for partisan motives, as if God were unambiguously on the side of capitalism and against any form of socialism. In fact, as we have emphasized from the beginning of these reflections, the unexpressed context for the TEN WORDS is the covenant with God, and this presupposes an ethic of solidarity. When applied to material possessions, solidarity turns into sharing. Any presumed "right" to property has meaning and justification solely in the wider setting of a society implicitly based on sharing. And in a society of sharing and mutual assistance, my sense of worth and security does not come from what I own but from the relationships I have with others. Greed therefore loses much of its venom, and theft its motivation.

For their part, the prophets of Israel already saw clearly the link between forgetting God and the breakdown of solidarity among God's people. Thousands of years before Karl Marx, they realized that grinding poverty and inequality were not natural givens but in large part consequences of human selfishness. In the eighth century BCE, the prophet Amos already described how some became poorer because others became richer:

> ...they sell the just for silver
> and the poor for a pair of sandals,
> longing to see the dust of the earth
> on the heads of the indigent,
> they thrust aside the way of the lowly.(...)
> Hear these words, cows of Bashan,
> grazing on the mountains of Samaria,
> oppressing the needy, crushing the poor....
>
> (Amos 2:6-7; 4:1)

A few centuries later, another prophet described the kind of worship pleasing to God:

> Is not this the sort of fast that pleases me:
> to break unjust fetters,
> to undo the cords of the yoke,
> to let the oppressed go free,
> to snap all yokes?
> Is it not to share your bread with the hungry,
> to give shelter to the homeless poor,

if you see naked persons, to cover them,
and not to abandon your own flesh and blood?

(Isaiah 58:6-7)

And in New Testament times, one of the early Christian leaders warned his flock against giving special treatment to those who were well off financially:

If a man with gold rings on his fingers, wearing expensive clothing, comes into your gathering, and a poor person dressed in filthy rags also comes in, and you take an interest in the one with fancy clothes and say to him, "Take that good seat there," while you say to the poor man, "You can stand here" or, "Sit at my feet," have you not practiced discrimination and become like corrupt judges? Listen, my dear brothers and sisters! Has not God chosen the poor of this world to make them rich in faith and heirs of the kingdom he promised to those who love him?     (James 2:2-5)

In the later history of the Christian Church, a similar notion of solidarity among all has always tempered any consideration of private ownership as an absolute right. Here is what Bishop Ambrose wrote to the affluent in fourth-century Milan:

It is not your possessions that you distribute to the poor; you are simply giving them back what belongs to them. For you have only kept for yourself what is given to all for the use of all. The earth belongs to all and not only to the rich, but it was expropriated by a

97

few to the detriment of all who work it. So, far from accomplishing acts of great generosity, you are only paying your debt.

(Naboth the Israelite, PL 14, 731-756)

Christian theologians have frequently stated that, in the hypothetical case of a poor man who takes bread from a rich man's table in order to keep himself and his family from starving, no theft has taken place. Or more exactly, a theft has indeed taken place, but it happened previously: the rich man's greed caused him to keep for himself what was superfluous for him but necessary for the survival of others. Even if his wealth was acquired by legal and honest means, his selfishness and failure to share breaks the divine covenant and contradicts the prohibition against stealing. It would not be a waste of time to ask ourselves whether the world as a whole today is not in certain respects similar to the example given above, if we are not living the parable of the rich man and Lazarus on a planetary scale (cf. Luke 16:19-21). If God protects the bond between human beings and their possessions, that can only be to make it possible for all to enjoy the good things of this earth and to know the happiness of sharing with others what one has been given.

You *will* not *give* false testimony
*against your* neighbor.

(Exodus 20:16 / Deuteronomy 5:20)

With this WORD, we shift to another level with respect to the three previous ones. They dealt with different forms of direct interaction between human beings, whereby God protects the essential aspects of existence by prohibiting us from violently taking another person's life, spouse or possessions. To make a society of freedom and happiness possible, human acts must be based on respect for the dignity of all. I am called to treat others as I wish to be treated myself.

The WORD we are now considering has the same aim, but at one degree removed from the previous ones. Let us begin by examining its literal meaning. In at least one respect, the world of biblical times was no different from our world today — disputes inevitably arose between individuals and groups regarding correct behavior. Two farmers, for instance, might both claim ownership of the same cow. If they were not able to decide the matter equitably among themselves, they would go to a public place ("the city gates"), where the most respected men of the town were to be found ("the elders") and expose the question to them. After examining the evidence and listening to relevant witnesses, these judges would render their verdict, which social pressure required the parties to respect.

Now this rudimentary but quite efficient juridical system made possible a kind of wrongdoing different in quality from that referred to in the previous three WORDS. Rather than directly stealing my neighbor's cow, I can lie to the judge or, better still, bribe someone else to testify that the animal in fact belongs to me, that he saw me purchase it from another. Giving false testimony is thus an indirect way of exercising violence upon others, by tampering with the laws that regulate human intercourse. Rather than using physical force or constraint to manipulate other human beings, it does violence to the representation of reality by which we orient ourselves in the world.

It should be clear upon reflection that this kind of wrongdoing, although less dramatic than outright murder or robbery, is in fact more insidious, because it demolishes the very foundations upon which a just society is built, the common understandings that make life together possible. Three thousand years ago, the prophets of Israel already understood that perverting the legal system opened the way to a society based on the law of the jungle, where the rich become richer and the poor ever poorer. An even more calamitous situation occurs when the judges themselves are corrupt, for then the wells are poisoned, and there is little hope for establishing justice. For this reason, a choice target of the prophets and those who followed in their footsteps were officials who did not use their authority to judge with integrity, but rather condoned wrongdoing for a price:

> I have found out the great number of your revolts
> and the enormity of your sins,
> trapping the innocent,
> taking a bribe
> and pushing away the poor at the city gate. (…)
> Your officials… love presents and run after gifts.
> They do not render a just verdict to the orphan
> and the widow's cause does not come before them. (…)
> They declare the guilty innocent for a bribe
> and deny justice to those without fault.
>
> (Amos 5:12; Isaiah 1:23; 5:23; cf. Psalm 82; 58)

The saying concerning false testimony, then, points beyond the prohibition of violent acts to the human representation of reality by language and other symbolic means. Pursuing a theme we have noticed several times already in our investigation of the TEN WORDS, it brings to light the vital importance of human language. Words can either be a means of being co-creators with God or else a source of de-creation, a way to exercise a subtle and destructive form of violence upon reality. An early Christian leader, following in the footsteps of the teachers of wisdom in Israel, understood the vital importance of human language both for good and for ill:

> When we put bits into the mouth of horses so that they will follow our lead, we control their whole body. And take sailing ships as another example: such large vessels, even when driven by strong winds, are controlled by a tiny rudder to go wherever the helmsman wishes. In the same way, the tongue is a tiny part of the body and boasts of great accomplishments. (…) With it we bless the Lord and Father, and with it we curse human beings made in the likeness of God. From the same mouth come blessings and curses.
>
> (James 3:3-5, 9-10; cf. Proverbs 15:4; 18:21; Sirach 5:13; 28:13-26)

The fact that the WORD regarding false testimony comes after a series dealing with different forms of misbehavior reveals a profound psychological truth. It witnesses to the fact that it is extremely difficult for human beings to do what they know to be wrong while admitting it, whether to themselves or to others. Wrongdoing is almost inevitably accompanied by a **denial** of the wrong done. We are possessed by the need to explain it away; we excuse our behavior, alleging special circumstances, exceptional pressures, placing our misdeeds or omissions in a context that makes them seem justified or at least inevitable. In short, we create an unreal world parallel to the real one, and in many cases, this violence done to reality is a greater wrong than the original infraction.

Thus the greatest power of human beings, that of taking part in the creation of a world mediated by language, is also our greatest trap. Imagination can widen our horizons, helping us to see new possibilities beyond the routines that close us in; it can also be a means to flee reality, or still worse, to imprison ourselves and others by creating a false universe that merely mirrors our self-image. The worst aspect of the counterfeit world we create by our untruth is that God is not present there. Since God is by definition ultimate Reality, when we leave reality behind for a mental construction of our own creation, by the very same act we exclude God from our lives. God cannot follow us into our self-created and self-centered world, which explains why such worlds oscillate between exaggerated hopes and utter despair.

Contemporary society is founded to an unprecedented degree on the mediation of reality through words, images and other symbolic means transmitted and amplified by technology. More than ever before in human history, we are insulated from a direct contact with things. We have even found a word, already mentioned in passing in these pages, to express this pseudo-creation of a parallel universe: we call it **virtual reality**. Here it needs to be emphasized once again that it is not the symbol-making faculty of human beings nor the power of their imagination that is the source of the problem; what is disastrous is losing the link between the "virtual" and the "real." When this is done intentionally we call it lying, but even when it is not fully intentional the effects are nonetheless serious. People today are bombarded by a host of representations through what is called the mass media, which transmit an implicit vision of what it means to be human. Many of these representations have only a very tenuous connection to the truth of our condition. The life they portray is inaccessible to almost everybody, and even if by some fairy godmother's magic wand such a life became possible, it would certainly not bring the happiness and fulfillment it seems to promise. And yet this "virtual reality" is seen by many of our contemporaries as more real than the life they are actually living, which in the final analysis fosters only disappointments, frustrations and emptiness. Glued to the screen, obstinately attempting to live in an unreal world, we cut ourselves off from the Source of true life and therefore from the possibility of finding authentic happiness.

In the Gospel according to Saint John, Jesus expresses clearly the link between violence against persons and violence against reality through words. Starting from the significant fact that his adversaries want to kill him because he has come to bear witness to the truth, which in John's Gospel refers to the reality about God and about human life, he explains:

> You have the devil for your father and want to accomplish the desires of your father. He was a murderer from the beginning and is not rooted in the truth, because there is no truth in him. When he tells a lie he is speaking according to his nature, because he is a liar and the father of lies. (John 8:44)

Evil personified in the figure of the Separator (**diabolos**) is both the enemy of life and the adversary of the truth, a murderer and a liar. With no roots in reality, indeed lacking true existence (for that would imply a communion of some sort with God), evil can only be destructive — and ultimately self-destructive. In the Book of Revelation, this relationship between the destruction of life and falsehood is shown in an even more dramatic fashion. The Dragon (*the Serpent of old, the devil or Satan,* Revelation 12:9) hands over his power to a beast who arises from the sea (13:1-2) to make war on God's people (13:7), and this first beast is seconded by another who arises from the earth and who uses his powers of persuasion to *make the earth and its inhabitants worship the first beast... [to] lead astray the inhabitants of the earth* (13:12,14). The two work hand-in-hand.

The two beasts can be seen as a reference to political power that rules directly by the sword and the spiritual authority that legitimates the claims of this power. On one level, then, we have here a perversion of the figures of the king and the prophet. At the time of Jesus' trial and execution, the two beasts would represent Pontius Pilate, on the one hand, symbolizing the political power of Rome, and on the other Caiaphas and the Jewish religious establishment which handed Jesus over to him. Today, in a world where organized religion in many cases no longer has the power to orient souls, we can legitimately ask whether the place of the second beast is not filled by what is called the mass media or the entertainment industry, when it makes use of all the tricks of technology to lead the public astray and to justify the aberrations of a society built on sand.

Another text from John's Gospel explains this connection by means of the symbolism of light and darkness:

> All who do evil hate the light and do not come into the light so that what they do may not be exposed. But those who act in truth come to the light, so that what they do may be clearly seen, since it has been done in God. (John 3:20-21)

As we approach the end of the second table of the TEN WORDS, then, the text focuses not on direct physical interaction between humans but on the justification of that interaction rooted in their symbol-making capacity, in other words in their ability to create a world mediated by meaning that either witnesses to the truth or disguises it for self-seeking ends. In this way God shows us that true freedom and happiness is possible only if we remain open to Reality, which always goes beyond what we can comprehend from our own limited standpoints. The logic of the Covenant is a permanent invitation to discover step by step all the dimensions of the Truth, which in the final analysis is identical with a universal communion.

You will not covet your neighbor's house.
You will not covet your neighbor's wife
and his male and female servant
and his ox and his donkey
and anything that belongs
to your neighbor.

(Exodus 20:17)


And you will not covet your neighbor's wife
And you will not desire your neighbor's house,
his field and his male and female slave,
his ox and his donkey
and anything that belongs
to your neighbor.

(Deuteronomy 5:21)

The final WORD (or WORDS: the version learned by Catholics and Lutherans, following Deuteronomy, distinguishes between the neighbor's wife and his other "possessions," whereas the Orthodox, Reformed and Jewish traditions treat this verse as a single WORD) poses a particular problem of interpretation. It is hard to see what it adds to what has come before. As a result, some Bible scholars see it as a doublet, a repetition of themes already mentioned, ostensibly because it has come from an originally independent source. Others see the difference as having to do with the behavior referred to; they interpret this WORD as referring to all forms of self-centered behavior that do not go as far as explicit murder, adultery and theft.

The main trend of interpretation in both the Jewish and Christian traditions, however, has been to put the accent on the verb, which seems to denote an inner attitude as opposed to an outward act. We need to remember, though, that the Bible never separates the inner and outer dimensions of human beings. "Coveting" here cannot refer to a disposition that remains purely interior; the word indicates something that begins in the human heart and leads to actions in the outer world. To "covet my neighbor's cow," for example, would mean to do all I can to make the animal my own, and not just to wish that it belonged to me. Still, even with this caveat in mind, it would be true to say that this WORD does betray a shift of accent with respect to the previous ones. They are all concerned with behavior that is clearly visible and judicable by an outside observer, while the end of the TEN WORDS directs our attention to an inner process or attitude, visible only secondarily by its consequences in the outer world.

This leads to the following question: What is this reality within the human person that makes life together impossible, by leading to acts that destroy the fabric of a society based on solidarity and sharing? The question is vastly more complex than one might suspect at first sight. The generic translation of the verb used is "to desire," but since in the Bible the Hebrew word most often appears in a negative context, the more specific verb "to covet" would appear to capture the nuance more exactly. Is desire then blameworthy in itself? Biblical spirituality, so respectful of the created universe, never seems to take this road. If all that God created is good (Genesis 1:31), and if what is good is "enticing" or "attractive" (Genesis 2:9; 3:6), then it would be hard to say that human desire is fundamentally misguided or evil without calling into question God's own goodness and wisdom, which is at the root of all that exists.

Some have taken another tack and have tried to resolve the question by postulating a fundamental dualism which situates within the human heart two radically different desires, one for good and one for evil. Upon reflection, we are forced to recognize that this attempt at a solution does not do justice to all the dimensions of the question either. Some Scriptural texts, such as Psalm 1, might appear to lend support to this outlook, and the Jewish rabbis could speak of the good and evil inclinations (*yetzer ha-tov* and *yetzer ha-ra'*) in human beings, but are not such constructs essentially a projection backwards and inwards of the observable fact that in specific situations human beings choose either good or evil? The duality is valid insofar as it expresses the two sides of a real alternative linked to every judgment of value. But reducing the "two ways" to "two inclinations," rather than shedding light on the question, may simply reflect our inability to understand evil and its origins. The unreflective genius of language seems to take us further: the Hebrew verb *hamad*, as well as the Greek *epithumeô*, the Latin *concupiscere* and the English "to covet," all vacillate between two meanings, to desire strongly and to desire wrongly. It is as if it is impossible to distinguish adequately between desire taken in itself and desire as the source of evil acts.

Even if no definitive distinction can be made, can we not attempt to understand better what comes about when the mere longing for something shifts to the propensity for wrongdoing? The first clue concerns the **intensity** of the desire. To covet something is to feel an immoderate yearning for it, not immoderate in an absolute sense, but rather in proportion to the object of the desire. The thing or person coveted seems absolutely necessary to our happiness, to such an extent that the frustration of not possessing it is intolerable; we are ready to do anything, infringe any prohibition, in order to achieve our end. In fact, the desired object has taken on a divine aura, and this explains why the Letter to the Colossians calls covetousness a form of idolatry (Colossians 3:5). In this sense, the end of the TEN WORDS echoes the beginning: God alone is to be worshiped, in other words God alone is the fitting object of unrestricted human desire. All other objects of our longing either satisfy limited needs or appetites, or should point beyond themselves to a greater longing. When they are turned into absolutes, they lead the dynamism of the human spirit astray. Our call to the universal is frustrated, and our hearts become divided and scattered when the part is taken for the whole.

And this brings us to the other way in which desire can be perverted. When such a totalitarian and misdirected desire takes

hold of the self, it causes us to ignore the legitimate claims —
and even the very existence — of our fellow human beings. Although the WORD we are examining speaks about our
**neighbor's** spouse or possessions, when we are blinded by a self-
centered desire, the other person is no longer seen as our neighbor, but as a rival for the same good. We cannot bear that another person may enjoy something that appeals to us; we cannot rejoice in his or her good fortune. Envy and jealousy have
taken the place of fellow feeling. The law of solidarity and sharing, so fundamental to the good life as defined by the covenant
with God, is undermined at its very roots.

To describe it in a more synthetic way, covetousness is a
desire which is experienced as a need, along the lines of hunger
or the sexual drive. This explains the imperious, life-or-death
quality of the feeling, as well as the impulse to possess — or indeed to incorporate — the object. This confusion of levels means
that what is noblest in human beings, their yearning for greater
life, the basic dynamism of their spirit, can be perverted into a
destructive force that makes a truly human existence impossible,
leaving division and devastation in its wake. It may seem simpler to speak of a penchant for both good and evil within us,
but both the tragedy and the hope of our condition is that the
two cannot be clearly distinguished. The same longing which
leads to what is most precious in life, a communion with God
and with our fellows, makes possible the worst, when it settles
for less than its true goal.

If all this seems excessively abstract, let us flesh it out by
looking at two concrete examples we find in the Bible. They both
concern kings of Israel. The first one is the great King David. In
chapter 11 of the Second Book of Samuel, we read that David
falls for a beautiful woman called Bathsheba. The king could have

had any of the unmarried women in his kingdom as wife or concubine, but his desire, blind to the claims of reality, is enflamed by one who is already married. He takes her and then, to hide his sin, has her husband killed. The story is a striking depiction of the spiral of evil, which begins with an imperious desire that knows no bounds.

The second example is found in chapter 21 of the First Book of Kings. King Ahab desires a plot of ground belonging to a man named Naboth. When Naboth refuses to sell him the plot, the queen has Naboth put to death on trumped-up grounds. In this case, covetousness leads to false witness, murder and theft. It is not insignificant that both of these examples of desire that entices to sin concern kings. Of all the men and women that people the Bible, kings are the most powerful; more like gods than mere human beings in the outlook of the ancient world, they possess almost everything they could possibly want or need. And yet in these stories, it is precisely the one thing forbidden that the king longs for most — this particular woman, that tiny plot of ground. The stories thus bear witness to a remarkable psychological insight, namely that in the final analysis, the source of evil is not a desire for this or that object but a desire to be "above the law," to have **everything.** The great temptation, especially for a king, is to see himself as "like God," bound by nobody or nothing. In fact this is a caricature, for the living God we meet in the pages of the Bible is not the one who possesses everything, but the one who shares everything out of love. Thus the king wishes not to be like God as God is in reality, but as he (wrongly) imagines God to be! The totalitarian desire we are warned against at the end of the TEN WORDS is therefore a projection onto God of human self-centeredness, as if God were the biggest Self of all and thus the most selfish. It is the ultimate idolatry and, as a result, the most effective obstacle to knowledge of the true and living God. In setting up a barrier to an unrestricted desire rooted in the maintenance of the self, the TEN WORDS attempt to keep open a space where the discovery of communion is possible.

Once again, we have here a suggestive parallel to the account of Adam and Eve in the first chapters of Genesis. The humans are free to eat the fruit of **all** the trees in the garden (Genesis 2:16). God holds back one tree alone, and it is that tree which becomes the locus of the temptation. The Tempter explains that by eating the fruit of precisely that tree and thus being bound by no law (see note, p. 13), the humans will be like God. According to the serpent, then, being like God means listening solely to the promptings of self, with no need to take the Other into account; the implicit ideal is thus a world with no others, a world where the deified self reigns supreme.

The second table of the TEN WORDS begins by proscribing outward behavior that destroys the bonds of solidarity and sharing with one's covenant partners and thus makes impossible freedom and happiness for all. At the end of this section, the accent shifts to the roots of such behavior within the human being. In so doing, it makes visible the unity between the two tables. What we call idolatry and covetousness are two expressions of the same fundamental error: taking the part for the whole, treating a created reality as the Source of all that is real, the key to perfect happiness. Looked at in another way, it means confusing the desire for God which calls us out of a settled existence with the satisfaction of presumed needs that shore up the self and ensure its survival. It means imagining the goal of existence not as the continual passage through deaths to self towards new life, but as a holding on at all costs to what we already have, as a false and unchanging eternity rooted in the denial of death.

Because of this progression within the text, the TEN WORDS mark out a space that is fundamentally open and incomplete. This open character was already manifest in the fact that almost all of the words are negative; they do not tell us **how** to live, but simply mark the boundaries within which authentic living is possible. But at the end, it becomes clear that outward behavior by itself can never solve the problem of happiness and freedom. Outward acts are rather the consequence of something more fundamental, which the text does no more than hint at by speaking of human desire. It thus asks a question to which it gives no exhaustive answer, and in this way opens up a field for further searching. The TEN WORDS point beyond themselves to a future development, and so the followers of Jesus are justified in seeing his teaching not as a contradiction of what went before but as a making explicit and a deepening of what was left unsaid. It is therefore appropriate to close our reflections with an investigation of the relationship between the TEN WORDS and the New Testament.

# Jesus and the Ten Words

In these pages, we have read the text known as the Ten Commandments or the TEN WORDS as defining a space of freedom that follows from the covenant with God. The God of the Bible calls his people out of an existence in slavery and opens a new life before them, a life which makes possible happiness and fulfillment for all. God's Word does not give an exhaustive definition of this new society, but simply the bare bones — the outlines which then have to be filled in by the creativity and responsibility of each hearer. It is thus fitting that at the end, the text shifts its focus from specific acts which destroy the fabric of life with others to the inner attitudes or mechanisms whereby human beings leave reality behind to set up a parallel world which is not in harmony with the intentions of the Creator. The teaching of Jesus, collected in the books that form what Christians call the New Testament, takes this reflection further, as well as showing a way out of the impasse created when human beings get lost in an unreal world.

At the beginning of the Gospel according to Saint Matthew, Jesus sums up the essential of his teaching, in Hebrew his Torah, in a long discourse traditionally known as the Sermon on the Mount (Matthew 5-7). The gospel-writer has undoubtedly compiled material from different times and places to create a coherent whole which functions as a kind of programmatic statement or manifesto. In this discourse, Jesus refers several times to the TEN WORDS. At first glance, his treatment of what the tradition has bequeathed to him may surprise or even shock us. It seems to call into question our image of the carpenter's son from Nazareth as a man of compassion, full of understanding for human weakness. Indeed, far from watering down the divine injunctions or minimizing their importance or relevance, Jesus instead radicalizes them beyond what seems to be the bounds of possibility:

> You have heard that it was said to your ancestors: You shall not commit murder; whoever commits murder will be subject to judgment. But I say to you: Whoever is angry with their brother or sister will be subject to judgment. Whoever calls their brother or sister an idiot will have to go before the supreme court. And whoever says, "You stupid fool," will deserve to be sent to the fiery pit. (…) You have heard that it was said: You shall not commit adultery. But I say to you: anyone who looks at a woman with lust has already committed adultery with her in his heart.
>
> (Matthew 5:21-22, 27-28)

Our first reaction upon hearing such words might well be to say, like the disciples in another context, *"If that is the case, then who can be saved?"* (cf. Matthew 19:25). Can anyone actually live in such a way as to fulfill God's Law? And indeed, that has been one of the ways these words of Jesus have been understood. According to this interpretation, Jesus radicalizes the commandments in order to show that nobody is capable of putting them into practice properly. In the face of God's claims, we all come up short. The commandments merely serve to convict us of our own sinfulness and our need to rely on the free gift of God's forgiving love, which comes to us through Jesus Christ.

While it is certainly true that, in Jesus' eyes, human beings cannot live according to God's will by their own efforts without divine assistance, it does not seem quite accurate to say that Jesus interprets the TEN WORDS in such a way as to make it impossible for anyone to put them into practice. His teaching in this respect is not merely negative; he is not only interested in having us discover our limits, but wants to point out a way forward. In the first place, Jesus is trying to tell his hearers something we have already discovered in the course of our investigation, namely, that it is not enough to follow the "letter" of the law in order to fulfill its basic intention. The fact that this morning we have not killed any of our neighbors, or robbed them, or committed adultery with their spouses, does not mean that we have done all that God intended in establishing a covenant with human beings. The TEN WORDS delineate the contours of the space of freedom defined by our relationship with God. To live lives according to the covenant, we must make use of the freedom we have received to build a society of solidarity and justice with God as its source, and to do this through all the concrete choices we make. In this respect, the text of the TEN WORDS is not an end but a beginning. It defines an orientation and indicates limits; it sets in motion a process that by its nature expands to include all the dimensions of our lives. As Jesus sees it, the smallest and seemingly most insignificant act we perform can be a means of putting the covenant with God into practice.

Secondly, Jesus' commentary on the TEN WORDS prolongs the end of that text by placing the accent not on outward behavior but on its roots within the human being. A key aspect of Jesus' teaching is that true religion cannot be merely a matter of outward compliance to written laws. The essential begins rather in the depths of human beings, in their fundamental attitude, which is then made concrete in choices that lead in turn to visible acts. The Bible refers to this core of the human person, from which the basic orientation comes, as the **heart**, and Jesus often emphasizes this characteristic structure of human activity in his teaching:

> And once again calling the crowd around him, he said to them: Listen to me, all of you, and get this into your head! There is nothing outside a person that can make them unclean by entering him. No, what comes **out** of a person is what makes that person unclean. (...) For it is from within, from a person's heart, that evil designs come forth: sexual immorality, thievery, murder (...). All these evil things come out of a person and make that person unclean.
>
> (Mark 7:14-15, 21-23)

This does not mean, as many of our contemporaries might think, that all that matters is my inner motivation, regardless of how I actually live. Jesus does not separate the inner and the outer; our basic orientation will determine the way we live in the world we share with others. To express this truth, he employs a simple image:

> No good tree produces rotten fruit, nor does a rotten tree produce good fruit. Every tree is known by the fruit it produces. You do not pick figs from a thornbush, nor gather grapes from briers. Good people bring forth what is good from the good treasure of

their hearts, and evil people bring forth evil from the evil within them. The mouth speaks when the heart overflows. (Luke 6:43-45)

In one way or another, sooner or later, the tree will bear fruit that reveals what kind of tree it is. *There is nothing hidden that will not come to light...* (Luke 8:17). If the roots buried underground are important, that is because they ultimately have visible consequences on the surface. The goal remains that of building a world where human beings live in harmony among themselves and with all of creation, but Jesus sees with unparalleled clarity that this project finds its origins in the secret places of the human heart.

And here we come finally to the basic problem with the TEN WORDS, and indeed with all of the divine commandments. This difficulty was present from the beginning of God's self-revelation, and now Jesus' teaching brings it into full focus. It can be expressed in a simple sentence: **Defining the ideal society does not bring it about.** It is not enough to tell people, "If you want to be free and happy, you must live in this way," for this to happen. This general statement finds ample confirmation in the history of the human race, and more specifically in the history of Israel as recounted in the Hebrew Scriptures. God may well have revealed his intentions to those he liberated from slavery and guided toward a land of promise, and indicated to them the road that led there; nonetheless, from the very beginning they tended to neglect the divine teaching, preferring to follow instead their own limited and ultimately futile ends. Instead of abandoning them, however, God continued to send men and women to call them back to the road of salvation, to remind them of the covenant and its requirements. These are the people we call the prophets, whose essential task was not to predict the future but to recall the covenant with God and to make clear to the nation the promises it contained and the consequences of neglecting it. And yet, more often than not, their message was not heeded either. The followers of Jesus were aware of this, and used this reading of history to try and awaken their contemporaries to a deeper understanding of their faith. In the Acts of the Apostles, a believer named Stephen, before being put to death for bearing witness to Christ, gave a long speech to the Jewish council of elders in which he outlined the history of salvation, concluding with these words:

> Stiff-necked and uncircumcised in heart and ears, you always resist the Holy Spirit just as your ancestors did! Was there ever a prophet they did not persecute? And they killed those who foretold the coming of the Righteous One, of whom you now have become betrayers and murderers; you received the Law from the hands of angels and have not kept it.    (Acts 7:51-53)

Stephen's words here echo those of Jesus himself when he apostrophizes the capital city, symbol of the "establishment": *you that kill the prophets and stone those sent to you* (Matthew 23:37). Those who come in God's name do not generally receive a warm welcome, even though later on people may revere them and build impressive tombs in their honor (Matthew 23:29). In short, it is clearly not enough to tell people how to follow God's way for it to become a reality that is put into practice.

Of all the prophets, it is Jeremiah whose writings show us

most clearly the resistance to the prophetic message and its consequences for the prophet himself. Seemingly a gentle man, he is called by God to proclaim forceful words which are like a fire burning in his heart; he cannot hold them back (Jeremiah 20:9). His call to the nation to change its ways leads only to his exclusion (Jeremiah 15:17) and persecution (Jeremiah 11:19, 21). Finally, he comes to realize that mere verbal persuasion will never cause his fellows to return to God, and he expresses this insight in a powerful and chilling image:

> Judah's sin is written with an iron pen,
> with a diamond point,
> engraved on the tablet of their hearts....
>
> (Jeremiah 17:1)

If sin — unfaithfulness to God — is what is written on the people's hearts, then it is futile to imagine that anything inscribed on tables of stone or proclaimed by others can modify their behavior. Jeremiah sees that, in the final analysis, his contemporaries will inevitably follow their inner promptings, not an appeal from without. This realization brings him close to despair:

> The heart is more deceitful than anything, incorrigible;
> who can fathom it?　　　　　(Jeremiah 17:9)

Because of this aspect of the human condition, God's Word in general, and the TEN WORDS in particular, become "law" in the negative and common understanding of the term, an external ideal with nothing that permits one to achieve it, a barrier that attempts to hold back the spontaneous dynamism of the human person and in the long run creates an intolerable situation. One attempts to obey the law at the cost of feeling trapped and frustrated until finally one succumbs to temptation, "breaking" the law and experiencing guilt and a sense of failure. In the long run, one may react against this unbearable state of affairs by attempting to throw off the yoke of the law entirely. In this scenario, as opposed to what we have been claiming in these pages from the beginning, personal freedom and happiness appear incompatible with an existence that tries to take seriously the Word of God.

The reasoning we have just sketched out parallels the main theme of St. Paul's Letter to the Romans. The apostle argues that, given the human condition as it is, salvation (in our terms freedom and happiness) cannot be achieved by following a written law. What makes this impossible is not any flaw in the law itself, but rather a split within human beings. Our hearts are divided:

> We know that the Law is spiritual. But I am the one who is unspiritual, sold as a slave to sin. For I do things I do not understand; I do not do what I want; instead I do what I hate. (…) I do not do the good that I want to do, but the evil that I do not want to do. (…) I take pleasure in God's Law in my innermost being, but I see another law at work in myself waging war against the law in my mind and making me a prisoner of the law of sin which motivates my actions.
>
> (Romans 7:14-15, 19, 22-23)

For the apostle, this is not merely abstract reasoning. Paul passes in review the history of humanity, concluding that not only pagans but even Jews, who have benefitted from God's direct revelation and therefore "know better," have been unable to live consistently according to God's will (Romans 2:1-3:20). And yet for Paul this in no way implies that the Torah, God's revealed Word, is at fault.

> What then are we saying? That the Law is sin? Absolutely not! But I only came to know sin through the Law. For I would not have known what coveting was had the Law not said: You shall not covet. (...) So the Law is holy, and the commandment holy and just and good. (...) But sin, so that it might appear as sin, produced death in me through something good, so that as a result of the commandment sin might be unambiguously revealed as sinful.          (Romans 7:7, 12, 13)

It was indeed a great gift that God revealed his will to humankind by means of the Torah. But if this gift by itself did not bring about the ideal society to which it aspired, this "failure" was providential insofar as it brought clearly to light just where the problem lay. In addition, seen in retrospect, it pointed forward to a further necessary step in God's self-disclosure which would have to be taken. God had already allowed his servant Jeremiah to glimpse this further step in a revelation that came to him at the heart of his despair. When the prophet lamented that the human heart was perverse and asked rhetorically who could fathom it, the response to his own question welled up in him:

I, the Lord, plumb the heart,
examine the sentiments,
and give to each one according to their behavior,
according to the fruit of their deeds.

(Jeremiah 17:10)

God, the creator of the human heart, is the only one able
to plumb its depths, and consequently the only one able to transform it. One day, Jeremiah received word of this future transformation which would finally solve the problem of the covenant
and the law:

The days are coming, says the Lord,
when I will make a new covenant
with the House of Israel and the House of Judah.
It will not be like the covenant
I made with their ancestors
on the day when I took them by the hand
and brought them out of the land of Egypt.
They broke that covenant,
though I was their Master, says the Lord.
No, this is the covenant I will make
with the House of Israel after those days,
says the Lord.
I will put my teaching within them
and write it on their hearts.
I will be their God
and they will be my people.
No longer will a man teach his companion
or a man his brother, saying:

Know the Lord!
For they will all know me,
from the least to the greatest, says the Lord,
for I will forgive their evildoing
and will remember their sins no longer.

(Jeremiah 31:31-34)

The only way out of the dilemma of a written law that cannot save is by a divine initiative which involves a total re-creation of the human heart, henceforth docile to God's promptings. Instead of sin being written on the heart, which sets it in fundamental opposition to God's desires, in this new dispensation God's Word will be an inner source of activity, with the result that human beings will follow spontaneously the path for which they were created. No dichotomy will then exist between what God wills for his creatures and their own understanding and intentions. At the same time the problem of freedom will be solved, since the divine commandments, now identified with the inner dynamism constitutive of human beings, will not evoke feelings of constraint or obligation.

Jeremiah described this new situation as a time when God's Torah, his teaching or law, would be written on the human heart. A generation later, a prophet called Ezekiel took up the same notion while changing the image:

I will sprinkle clean water on you and make you clean.
I will purify you from all your uncleanness and all your
idols. I will give you a new heart and put a new breath
of life within you. I will take out of your bodies your
heart of stone and give you a human heart. And I will

put my breath of life in you and make you follow my
decrees and keep my laws. You will live in the land I
gave to your ancestors, and you will be my people and
I will be your God.                    (Ezekiel 36:25-28)

This prophet describes the change as one of receiving a
completely new heart — an authentically human heart that replaces one which was incapable of hearing and acting in consequence. And he speaks of this transformation as a new creation,
the work of God's own life-force or Spirit, henceforth fully at
home within the human person. As for Jeremiah, the result of
this new creative initiative on God's part will be to remove any
disharmony between God and the people. From now on the two
will walk hand in hand: *You will be my people and I will be your
God.*

For the followers of Jesus, those who recognized him as *the
Christ, the Son of the living God* (Matthew 16:16; cf. Mark 1:1),
this harmony between God and humanity was not simply a hope
for the future; it had become a present reality. First of all in Jesus
himself, who came *not to do [his] own will but the will of the One
who sent [him]* (John 6:38; cf. 8:29). And afterwards in his followers, as shown above all in the event of the first Christian Pentecost, recounted by Luke in chapter 2 of the Acts of the
Apostles. Although Christians celebrate Pentecost as one of their
main religious feasts, few are aware that in the first place it was
— and is — a Jewish holy day. Also known as the Feast of Weeks
(Shavuoth), it is one of the three high holy days of the Jewish
calendar (cf. Exodus 23:14-17). Originally a harvest festival oc-
curring fifty days after Passover, it eventually became associated
in the memory of Israel with the events of the Exodus from

Egypt. In Exodus 19:1 we read that *in the third month after leaving Egypt, the Israelites came to the desert of Sinai.* The rabbis therefore interpreted Pentecost to refer to the day when Israel reached Sinai — fifty days includes the end of one month, the second month, and the beginning of the third. Shavuoth thus became the celebration of what happened on the holy mountain: the covenant with God made concrete in the gift of the Torah. Pentecost is the feast of the covenant, the remembrance of the gift of the Torah, and thus in a real sense the day of the TEN WORDS.

In the wake of the resurrection of Jesus, this day for remembering the past and making it present undergoes a transformation, so that for the followers of Christ it becomes a fulfillment of what went before and an authentic new beginning. Tongues of fire, identified with God's Breath of life, the Holy Spirit, come down upon the disciples gathered in the upper room. If we realize that, when the Jewish people recounted the events on Sinai, in some versions of the story it is said that God wrote the TEN WORDS on the tablets of stone with his finger, often identified by the rabbis as his Spirit, and in other versions with tongues of flame, then the link between the Hebrew and the Christian Pentecost becomes evident. Here God writes his Word, not on tablets of stone, but on the hearts of the faithful. The prophecy of Jeremiah, taken up by Ezekiel, has become a reality. By Jesus' self-giving and his rising from the dead, the covenant has become totally renewed. It is no longer mediated by an external reality, good in itself but foreign to the deepest dynamism of the human being, but rather by the presence of God's Spirit transforming human activity from within.

To understand fully the significance of the Christian Pentecost, it is also essential to realize that it was not merely a once-and-for-all event, something that happened two thousand years ago in Palestine. After the manifestation of the Spirit and Peter's explanation to the crowd of bystanders, they ask him what they should do. And Peter replies:

> Change your hearts, and each of you should be baptized in the name of Jesus Christ for the forgiveness of your sins, and you will receive the gift of the Holy Spirit. For the promise is meant for you and your children as well as for all who are far off, for as many as the Lord our God will call. (Acts 2:38-39)

What happened in Jerusalem was the epicenter of an earthquake that has continued to send its shock waves down through the ages. The Pentecost experience keeps on echoing in the lives of women and men in a host of times and places who hear the Good News of Jesus Christ and take it to heart. The new life into which they enter is recapitulated in the act of baptism.

This brings us to a final question, one that admits of no easy answer. Many, if not most Christians, could reason in the following way: "I am baptized, and try to live out my faith as best I can. But I do not have the impression that I accomplish God's will spontaneously. I still feel a tension within myself, the inner struggle of which Saint Paul spoke in chapter 6 of his Letter to the Romans between the good I want to do and the way I in fact live. So what has changed as a result of the coming of Christ? What does it mean concretely to have received the gift of the Holy Spirit as an 'inner law'?"

This question needs to be taken seriously. Obviously, if

there is no empirical change in the behavior of people who have opened themselves to the new life given by Christ, then it becomes hard to see what the language of the New Testament refers to. Jesus had already stated that it is by the love shown by Christians that others would recognize the truth of his message (cf. John 13:35; 17:21-23). What could a "law written in our hearts" possibly mean if we behave exactly the same way as people who know of no such law, and who attempt as best they can to live according to values they have received from the society in which they live? Christians have often spoken as if they were morally superior to members of other faiths, even though (or perhaps especially when) their behavior gave no tangible evidence of such superiority. Unwittingly, they are then making the same claims for which Saint Paul criticized his own fellow Jews:

> You have no excuse when you judge others. You condemn yourselves when you judge them, because you do the very same things you criticize in others. (...) You rely upon the Law and boast about your relationship to God. You claim to know God's will and to judge what is best because you are instructed by the Law, convinced that you are a guide for the blind, a light for those in the dark, an instructor of the ignorant, a teacher of the immature, having in the Law the epitome of knowledge and truth. Why, then, teaching others, do you not teach yourselves? (...) Bragging about the Law, why do you dishonor God by breaking the Law? (Romans 2:1, 17-21, 23)

To find a way out of this dilemma, we need to examine more closely the logic of God's acting. Because of an uncritical human understanding of God as "almighty," we tend to imagine that God can or should act like a magician who, with a wave of his wand, radically transforms our human reality in the blink of an eye. If this were the case, welcoming the Holy Spirit into our lives in baptism should lead to an immediate and total change of our lifestyle and behavior. Upon closer reflection, however, we can see that this is not the way things happen. God respects the structure and rhythms of the world he has created. Indeed, violating these would be a kind of self-contradiction on God's part. Slowly, with infinite patience, God works from within, calling human beings to an ever wider and more intimate communion with himself.

One Gospel image that can help us to grasp this process is that of a **seed**. In a key story or parable he employs to explain his teaching, Jesus compares the coming of God's Kingdom to a farmer casting seed on the ground, seed which grows in different ways according to the kind of soil into which it falls (Mark 4:2-9). Elsewhere, he describes the Kingdom as a tiny seed which becomes a large plant (Matthew 13:31-32). In his turn Peter, writing to some new Christians, tells them:

> You have been reborn not from a perishable seed but
> from an imperishable one, from the living and lasting
> Word of God. (1 Peter 1:23)

In other words, we can envision the "inner law" which is the presence of the Holy Spirit in our hearts as a tiny seed planted in us at baptism, a seed that needs to grow and develop until it transforms the whole of our existence. Christians are therefore not necessarily better people than those whose identity consists in the attempt faithfully to follow a written law; it is the **logic** of their behavior which is different. External manifestations, for example God's Word found in the Bible, do not regulate their actions so much as reflect what God is accomplishing within them. They use outward teaching as a kind of mirror that helps them better to grasp their inward transformation under the impulsion of the Holy Spirit. That is why Saint John can write to his disciples:

> As for you, you have an anointing from the Holy One, and you all have knowledge. (...) And since the anointing you have received from him remains in you, you do not need anyone to teach you, but since his anointing teaches you about everything, and since it is true and not a lie, remain in him just as it has taught you.                              (1 John 2:20, 27)

Naturally, Christians need to receive teaching from those who have gone before them. John himself, by writing these words, is in fact teaching those entrusted to his care. This teaching, however, serves not to give them something new but rather to awaken in them what is implicitly there "from the beginning" (cf. 1 John 1:1; 2:7, 24; 3:11), a beginning made concrete in their lives when they discovered a call from God and entered the community of believers. Its role is to draw out all the implications of the choice they have made — and the gift they have received — in agreeing to follow Christ. This, incidentally, is one of the main themes of the first letter of John: the essential task of believers is to remain faithful to what they received in the beginning; everything, that is to say, communion with the Father in Christ through the inner presence of the Holy Spirit, was given from the start, recapitulated in the yes of baptism, and by remaining faithful to this yes they will receive all they need to confront the new challenges and trials each day brings. And for John, the key sign of their faithfulness to what they received in the beginning is their active membership in the Christian community.

The TEN WORDS, then, do not cease to be valid for the followers of Jesus Christ. It is simply that the center of gravity has shifted from an outward law or command to an inner word heard and kept in the heart. This inner word indicates a direction to be followed in a constant process of deepening; it becomes what Saint James calls *the perfect Law of freedom* and which he identifies with *the Word which has been planted in you*, taking up for his part the image of the seed (James 1:25, 21).

The most important thing followers of Christ can do, therefore, is to trust in what the Spirit is accomplishing within them. The main question for us is not "What should we do?" nor even "How should we live?" but "How can we nourish the seed which has been planted within us?" By reading and meditating upon Scripture, through individual and communal prayer which has its focal point in the celebration of the Eucharist, by supporting one another as sisters and brothers in Christ, by living lives of self-giving, believers allow the new life rooted in them to blossom and bear fruit in abundance. At that point, they may discover something that the teachers of Israel had already noted many centuries ago. In the Hebrew language, a negative command is expressed not by the imperative mood but by a tense equivalent to the future indicative — not "Do not kill" but rather "You will not kill." Asking themselves why this was the case, the rabbis replied that the TEN WORDS were not so much a series of commands as a promise. By meditating on the Torah and taking it to heart, believers little by little become people who are truly in the image of their Creator, who live in the way God intends: "You will not kill." Here we are at the opposite extreme from a narrow legalistic outlook, so often attributed wrongly to the Jewish people. God's Word is a promise of life, pointing towards a world of freedom and happiness, where justice and peace reign. And for those who place their trust in Christ, this promise is not a mere object of future expectation. Through the coming of Jesus, his death and resurrection and the pouring out of the Spirit *without reserve* (John 3:34), it has become a permanent possibility in our present day: *all God's promises have found their yes in him* (2 Corinthians 1:20).

The power of the Gospel is also found in the Law, and
the Gospels become fully understandable when fixed on
the foundation of the Law. And I do not call it the "Old
Testament" if I understand it spiritually. The Law only
becomes an "Old Testament" for those who understand
it in a merely human fashion; of necessity it has become
old for them, since it cannot hold on to its vigor. But for
us, who understand and explain it in the Spirit and
according to the Gospel, it is always new. Both Testa-
ments are a New Testament for us, not because of their
chronological age but because of the newness of the way
they are understood.

> Origen, third-century Greek Christian
> thinker, in his *Homilies on Numbers* IX,4
> (Sources chrétiennes, 415)

ST PAULS

This book was produced by St. Pauls/Alba House, the Society of St. Paul, an international religious congregation of priests and brothers dedicated to serving the Church through the communications media.

For information regarding this and associated ministries of the Pauline Family of Congregations, write to the Vocation Director, Society of St. Paul, P.O. Box 189, 9531 Akron-Canfield Road, Canfield, Ohio 44406-0189. Phone (330) 702-0359; or E-mail: spvocationoffice@aol.com or check our internet site, www.albahouse.org